THE

Barbarism of Slavery.

[NEW EDITION—WITH A DEDICATION.]

BY

Hon. CHARLES SUMNER.

ISBN-13:
978-1497319707

ISBN-10:
1497319706

- Title: Charles Sumner, 1811-1874
- Date Created/Published: [no date recorded on caption card]
- Medium: 1 photographic print.
- Summary: Half lgth., seated, facing left.
- Reproduction Number: LC-USZ62-66840 (b&w film copy neg.)
- Rights Advisory: No known restrictions on publication.
- Call Number: BIOG FILE - Sumner, Charles, 1811-1874 [item] [P&P]
- Repository: Library of Congress Prints and Photographs Division Washington, D.C. 20540 USA

THE

BARBARISM OF SLAVERY:

SPEECH OF

Hon. Charles Sumner,

ON THE

Bill for the Admission of Kansas as a Free State,

In the United States Senate, June 4, 1860.

NEW EDITION—WITH A DEDICATION.

MR. MADISON THOUGHT IT WRONG TO ADMIT IN THE CONSTITUTION THE IDEA
OF PROPERTY IN MAN.—*Debates in the Federal Convention, 25th August,* 1787.

PUBLISHED BY

THE YOUNG MEN'S REPUBLICAN UNION.

(For Sale by John Bradburn, 49 Walker Street.)

NEW-YORK, 1863.

DEDICATION.

To the Young Men of the United States, I dedicate this new edition of a Speech on the Barbarism of Slavery, in token of heartfelt gratitude to them for brave and patriotic service rendered in the present War for Civilization:

It is now more than three years since I deemed it my duty to expose, in the Senate, the Barbarism of Slavery. This phrase, though common now, was new then. The speech was a strict and logical reply to the assumptions of Senators, asserting the "divine origin" of Slavery, its "ennobling" character, and that it was the "black marble keystone" of our national arch. Listening to these assumptions, which were of daily recurrence, I felt that they ought to be answered. And, considering their effrontery, it seemed to me that they should be answered frankly and openly by exhibiting Slavery *as it really is*, without reserve; careful that I should "nothing extenuate, nor set down aught in malice." This I did.

In that debate the issue was joined which is still pending in the Trial by Battle. The inordinate assumptions for Slavery naturally ripened in Rebellion and War. If Slavery were, in reality, all that it was said to be by its representatives, they must have failed in duty if they did not vindicate and advance it. Not easily could they see a thing so "divine" and so "ennobling"—constituting the "black marble keystone" of our national arch—discredited by a popular vote, even if not yet doomed to sacrifice.

The election of Mr. Lincoln was a judgment against Slavery, and its representatives were aroused.

Meanwhile, for more than a generation, an assumption of constitutional law, hardly less outrageous, had become rooted side by side with Slavery, so that the two had shot up in rank luxuriance together. It was assumed that any State was privileged, under the Constitution, at any time, in the exercise of its own discretion, to withdraw from the Union. This absurdity found little favor at first, even among the representatives of Slavery. To say that two and two make five could not be more irrational. But custom and constant repetition gradually produced an impression, until, at last, all who were maddest for Slavery were equally mad for this disorganizing ally.

It was under the shadow of this constitutional assumption that the assumption for Slavery grew into virulent vigor, so that, at last, when Mr. Lincoln was elected, it broke forth in open war; but the war was declared in the name of State Rights.

SPEECH.

———◆•◆———

MR. PRESIDENT: Undertaking now, after a silence of more than four years, to address the Senate on this important subject, I should suppress the emotions natural to such an occasion, if I did not declare on the threshold my gratitude to that Supreme Being, through whose benign care I am enabled, after much suffering and many changes, once again to resume my duties here, and to speak for the cause which is so near my heart. To the honored Commonwealth whose representative I am, and also to my immediate associates in this body, with whom I enjoy the fellowship which is found *in thinking alike concerning the Republic,* I owe thanks which I seize this moment to express for the indulgence shown me throughout the protracted seclusion enjoined by medical skill; and I trust that it will not be thought unbecoming in me to put on record here, as an apology for leaving my seat so long vacant, without making way, by resignation, for a successor, that I acted under the illusion of an invalid, whose hopes for restoration to his natural health constantly triumphed over his disappointments.

When last I entered into this debate, it became my duty to expose the Crime against Kansas, and to insist upon the immediate admission of that Territory as a State of this Union, with a Constitution forbidding Slavery. Time has passed; but the question remains. Resuming the discussion precisely where I left it, I am happy to avow that rule of moderation, which, it is said, may venture to fix the boundaries of wisdom itself. I have no personal griefs to utter; only a barbarous egotism could intrude these into this chamber. I have no personal wrongs to avenge; only a barbarous nature could attempt to wield that vengeance which belongs to the Lord. The years that have intervened, and the tombs that have been opened, since I spoke, have their voices too, which I can not fail

6

to hear. Besides, what am I—what is any man among the living or among the dead—compared with the Question before us? It is this alone which I shall discuss, and I open the argument with that easy victory which is found in charity.

The Crime against Kansas stands forth in painful light. Search history, and you can not find its parallel. The slave-trade is bad; but even this enormity is petty, compared with that elaborate contrivance by which, in a Christian age and within the limits of a Republic, all forms of constitutional liberty were perverted; by which all the rights of human nature were violated, and the whole country was held trembling on the edge of civil war; while all this large exuberance of wickedness, detestable in itself, becomes tenfold more detestable when its origin is traced to the madness for Slavery. The fatal partition between Freedom and Slavery, known as the Missouri Compromise; the subsequent overthrow of this partition, and the seizure of all by Slavery; the violation of plighted faith; the conspiracy to force Slavery at all hazards into Kansas; the successive invasions by which all security there was destroyed, and the electoral franchise itself was trodden down; the sacrilegious seizure of the very polls, and, through pretended forms of law, the imposition of a foreign legislature upon this Territory; the acts of this legislature, fortifying the Usurpation, and, among other things, establishing test-oaths, calculated to disfranchise actual settlers, friendly to Freedom, and securing the privileges of the citizen to actual strangers friendly to Slavery; the whole crowned by a statute—" the be-all and the end-all" of the whole Usurpation—through which Slavery was not only recognized on this beautiful soil, but made to bristle with a Code of Death such as the world has rarely seen; all these I have fully exposed on a former occasion. And yet the most important part of the argument was at that time left untouched; I mean that which is found in the Character of Slavery. This natural sequel, with the permission of the Senate, I propose now to supply.

Motive is to Crime as soul to body; and it is only when we comprehend the motive that we can truly comprehend the Crime. Here, the motive is found in Slavery and the rage for its extension. Therefore, by logical necessity, must Slavery be discussed; not indirectly, timidly, and sparingly, but directly, openly, and thoroughly. It must be exhibited as it is; alike in its influence and in its animating character, so that not only its outside but its inside may be seen.

This is no time for soft words or excuses. All such are out of place. They may turn away wrath; but what is the wrath of man? This is no time to abandon any advantage in the argument. Senators sometimes announce that they resist Slavery on political grounds only, and remind us that they say nothing of the moral question. This is wrong. Slavery must be resisted not only on political grounds, but on all other grounds, whether social, economical, or moral. Ours is no holiday contest; nor is it any strife of rival factions; of White and Red Roses; of theatric Neri and Bianchi; but it is a solemn battle between Right and Wrong; between Good and Evil. Such a battle can not be fought with excuses or with rose-water. There is austere work to be done, and Freedom can not consent to fling away any of her weapons.

If I were disposed to shrink from this discussion, the boundless assumptions now made by Senators on the other side would not allow me. The whole character of Slavery as a pretended form of civilization is put directly in issue, with a pertinacity and a hardihood which banish all reserve on this side. In these assumptions, Senators from South-Carolina naturally take the lead. Following Mr. Calhoun, who pronounced "Slavery the most safe and stable basis for free institutions in the world," and Mr. McDuffie, who did not shrink from calling it "the cornerstone of the republican edifice," the Senator from South-Carolina [Mr. HAMMOND] insists that "its forms of society are the best in the world;" and his colleague [Mr. CHESNUT] takes up the strain. One Senator from Mississippi [Mr. DAVIS] adds, that Slavery "is but a form of civil government for those who are not fit to govern themselves;" and his colleague [Mr. BROWN] openly vaunts that it "is a great moral, social, and political blessing—a blessing to the slave, and a blessing to the master." One Senator from Virginia, [Mr. HUNTER,] in a studied vindication of what he is pleased to call "the social system of the slaveholding States," exalts Slavery as "the normal condition of human society," "beneficial to the non-slave-owner as it is to the slave-owner," "best for the happiness of both races;" and, in enthusiastic advocacy, declares, "that the very keystone of the mighty arch, which by its concentrated strength is able to sustain our social superstructure, consists in the black marble block of African Slavery. Knock that out," he says, "and the mighty fabric, with all that it upholds, topples and tumbles to its fall." These were his very words, uttered in debate here. And his colleague, [Mr. MASON,] who has never hesitated where Slavery was in question, has proclaimed that it is "*ennobling* to both master and slave"—a word which, so far as the slave was concerned, he changed, on a subsequent day, to "elevating," assuming still that it is "ennobling" to the master—which is simply a new version of an old assumption, by Mr. McDuffie, of South-Carolina, that "Slavery supersedes the necessity of an order of nobility."

Thus, by various voices, is the claim made for Slavery, which is put forward defiantly as a form of civilization—as if its existence were not plainly inconsistent with the first principles of any thing that can be called Civilization—except by that figure of speech in classical literature, where a thing takes its name from something which it has not, as the dreadful Fates were called merciful because they were without mercy. And pardon the allusion, if I add, that, listening to these sounding words for Slavery, I am reminded of the kindred extravagance related by that remarkable traveler in China, the late Abbé Huc, of a gloomy hole in which he was lodged, pestered by mosquitoes and exhaling noisome vapors, where light and air entered only by a single narrow aperture, but styled by Chinese pride the Hotel of the Beatitudes.

It is natural that Senators thus insensible to the true character of Slavery, should evince an equal insensibility to the true character of the Constitution. This is shown in the claim now made, and pressed with unprecedented energy, degrading the work of our fathers, that by virtue of the Constitution, the pretended property in man is placed beyond the reach of Congressional prohibition even within Congressional jurisdiction, so that the Slave-master may at all times enter the broad outlying Territories of the Union with the victims of his oppression, and there continue to hold them by lash and chain.

Such are the two assumptions, the *first* an assumption of fact, and the *second* an assumption of constitutional law, which are now made without apology or hesitation. I meet them both.

To the first I oppose the essential Barbarism of Slavery, in all its influences, whether high or low, as Satan is Satan still, whether towering in the sky or squatting in the toad. To the second I oppose the unanswerable, irresistible truth, that the Constitution of the United States nowhere recognizes property in man. These two assumptions naturally go together. They are "twins" suckled by the same wolf. They are the "couple" in the present slave-hunt. And the latter can not be answered without exposing the former. It is only when Slavery is exhibited in its truly hateful character, that we can fully appreciate the absurdity of the assumption, which, in defiance of the express letter of the Constitution, and without a single sentence, phrase, or word, upholding human bondage, yet foists into this blameless text the barbarous idea that man can hold property in man.

On former occasions, I have discussed Slavery only incidentally; as, in unfolding the principle that Slavery is Sectional and Freedom National; in exposing the unconstitutionality of the Fugitive Slave Bill; in vindicating the Prohibition of Slavery in the Missouri Territory; in exhibiting the imbecility throughout the Revolution of the Slave States, and especially of South-Carolina; and lastly, in unmasking the Crime against Kansas. On all these occasions, where I have spoken at length, I have said too little of the character of Slavery, partly because other topics were presented, and partly from a disinclination which I have always felt to press the argument against those whom I knew to have all the sensitiveness of a sick man. But, God be praised, this time has passed, and the debate is now lifted from details to principles. Grander debate has not occurred in our history, rarely in any history; nor can this debate close or subside except with the triumph of Freedom.

FIRST ASSUMPTION.—Of course I begin with the assumption of fact.

It was the often-quoted remark of John Wesley, who knew well how to use words, as also how to touch hearts, that Slavery was " the sum of all villainies." The phrase is pungent; but it would be rash in any of us to criticise the testimony of that illustrious founder of Methodism, whose ample experience of Slavery in Georgia and the Carolinas seems to have been all condensed in this sententious judgment. Language is feeble to express all the enormity of this institution, which is now vaunted as in itself a form of civilization, "ennobling" at least to the master, if not to the slave. Look at it in whatever light you will, and it is always the scab, the canker, the "bare-bones," and the shame of the country; wrong, not merely in the abstract, as is often admitted by its apologists, but wrong in the concrete also, and possessing no single element of right. Look at it in the light of principles, and it is nothing less than a huge insurrection against the eternal law of God, involving in its pretensions the denial of all human rights, and also the denial of that Divine Law in which God himself is manifest, thus being practically the grossest lie and the grossest Atheism. Founded in violence, sustained only by violence, such a wrong must by a sure law of compensation blast the master as well as the slave; blast the lands on which they live; blast the community of which they are a part; blast the Government which does not forbid the outrage; and the longer it exists and the more completely it prevails, must its blasting influences penetrate the whole social system. Barbarous in origin; barbarous in its law; barbarous in all its pretensions; barbarous in the instruments it employs; barbarous in consequences; barbarous in spirit; barbarous wherever it shows itself, Slavery must breed Barbarians, while it develops everywhere, alike in the individual and in the society to which he belongs, the essential elements of Barbarism. In this character it is now conspicuous before the world.

In undertaking now to expose the BARBARISM OF SLAVERY, the whole broad field is open before me. There is nothing in its character, its manifold wrong, its wretched results, and especially in its influence on the class who claim to be "ennobled" by it, that will not fall naturally under consideration.

I know well the difficulty of this discussion involved in the humiliating Truth with which I begin. Senators on former occasions, revealing their sensibility, have even protested against any comparison between what were called the "two civilizations," meaning the two social systems produced respectively by Freedom and by Slavery. The sensibility and the protest are not unnatural, though mistaken. "Two civilizations!" Sir, in this nineteenth century of Christian light, there can be but one Civilization, and this is where Freedom prevails. Between Slavery and Civilization there is an essential incompatibility. If you are for the one, you can not be for the other; and just in proportion to the embrace of Slavery is the divorce from Civilization. That Slave-masters should be disturbed when this is exposed, might be expected. But the assumptions now so boastfully made, while they may not prevent the sensibility, yet surely exclude all ground of protest when these assumptions are exposed.

Nor is this the only difficulty. Slavery is a bloody Touch-me-not, and everywhere in sight now blooms the bloody flower. It is on the wayside as we approach the national capital; it is on the marble steps which we mount; it flaunts on this floor. I stand now in the house of its friends. About me while I speak are its most sensitive guardians, who have shown in the past how much they are ready either to do or not to do where Slavery is in question. Menaces to deter me have not been spared. But I should ill deserve this high post of duty here, with which I have been honored by a generous and enlightened people, if I could hesitate. Idolatry has been often exposed in the presence of idolaters, and hypocrisy has been chastised in the presence of Scribes and Pharisees. Such examples may give encouragement to a Senator who undertakes in this presence to expose Slavery; nor can any language, directly responsive to the assumptions now made for this Barbarism, be open to question. Slavery can only be painted in the sternest colors; but I cannot forget that nature's sternest painter has been called the best.

The BARBARISM OF SLAVERY appears; *first* in the *character of Slavery*, and *secondly* in the *character of Slave-masters*. Under the first head we shall naturally consider (1) the Law of Slavery and its Origin, and (2) the practical results of Slavery as shown in a comparison between the Free States and the Slave States. Under the *second* head we shall naturally consider (1) Slave-masters as shown in the Law of Slavery; (2) Slave-masters in their relations with slaves, here glancing at their three brutal instruments; (3) Slave-masters in their relations with each other, with society, and with Government; and (4) Slave-masters in their unconsciousness.

The way will then be prepared for the consideration of the assumption of constitutional law.

12

I. In presenting the CHARACTER OF SLAVERY, there is little for me to do, except to allow Slavery to paint itself. When this is done, the picture will need no explanatory words.

(1.) I begin with the *Law of Slavery and its Origin*, and here this Barbarism paints itself in its own chosen definition. It is simply this: Man, created in the image of God, is divested of his human character, and declared to be a "chattel"—that is, a beast, a thing or article of property. That this statement may not seem to be put forward without precise authority, I quote the statutes of three different States, beginning with South-Carolina, whose voice for Slavery always has an unerring distinctiveness. Here is the definition supplied by this State:

"Slaves shall be deemed, held, taken, reputed, and adjudged in law, to be *chattels personal* in the hands of their owners and possessors and their executors, administrators, and assigns, to all intents, constructions, and purposes whatsoever."— *2 Brev. Dig.*, 229.

And here is the definition supplied by the Civil Code of Louisiana:

"A slave is one who is in the power of a master to whom he belongs. The master may sell him, dispose of his person, his industry, and his labor. He can do nothing, possess nothing, nor acquire any thing, but what must belong to his master."—*Civil Code, Art.* 35.

In similar spirit, the law of Maryland thus indirectly defines a slave as an *article:*

"In case the personal property of a ward shall consist of specific *articles, such as slaves*, working beasts, animals of any kind, the court, if it deem it advantageous for the ward, may at any time pass an order for the sale thereof."—*Statutes of Maryland*.

Not to occupy time unnecessarily, I present a summary of the pretended law defining Slavery in all the Slave States, as made by a careful writer, Judge Stroud, in a work of juridical as well as philanthropic merit:

"The cardinal principle of Slavery—that the slave is not to be ranked among *sentient* beings, but among *things*—is an article of property—a chattel personal—obtains as undoubted law in all of these (Slave) States."—*Stroud's Law of Slavery.* *p.* 22.

Out of this definition, as from a solitary germ, which in its pettiness might be crushed by the hand, towers our Upas Tree and all its gigantic poison. Study it, and you will comprehend the whole monstrous growth.

Sir, look at its plain import, and see the relation which it establishes. The slave is held simply *for the use of his master*, to whose behests, his life, liberty, and happiness are devoted, and by whom he may be bartered, leased, mortgaged, bequeathed, invoiced, shipped as cargo, stored as goods, sold on execution, knocked off at public auction, and even staked at the gaming-table on the hazard of a card or a die; all according to law. Nor is there any thing, within the limit of life, inflicted on a beast which may not be inflicted on the slave. He may be marked like a hog, branded like a mule, yoked like an ox, hobbled like a horse, driven like an ass, sheared like a sheep, maimed like a cur, and constantly beaten like a brute; all according to law. And should life itself be taken, what is the remedy? The Law of Slavery, imitating that rule of evidence which, in barbarous days and barbarous countries, prevented a Christian from testi-fying against a Mohammedan, openly pronounces the incompe-tency of the whole African race—whether bond or free—to tes-tify in any case against a white man, and, thus having already surrendered the slave to all possible outrage, crowns its tyranny, by excluding the very testimony through which the bloody cruelty of the Slave-master might be exposed.

Thus in its Law does Slavery paint itself; but it is only when we look at details, and detect its essential elements—*five in num-ber*—all inspired by a *single motive*, that its character becomes completely manifest.

Foremost, of course, in these elements, is the impossible pre-tension, where Barbarism is lost in impiety, by which man claims *property in man*. Against such arrogance the argument is brief. According to the law of nature, written by the same hand that placed the planets in their orbits, and like them, constituting a part of the eternal system of the Universe, every human being has a complete title to himself direct from the Almighty. Naked he is born; but this birthright is inseparable from the human form. A man may be poor in this world's goods; but he owns himself. No war or robbery, ancient or recent; no capture; no middle passage; no change of clime; no purchase-money; no transmis-sion from hand to hand, no matter how many times, and no matter at what price, can defeat this indefeasible God-given fran-chise. And a divine mandate, strong as that which guards Life, guards Liberty also. Even at the very morning of Cre-ation, when God said, let there be Light—earlier than the male-diction against murder—He set an everlasting difference between man and a chattel, giving to man dominion over the fish of the

14

sea, and over the fowl of the air, and over every living thing that moveth upon the earth :

> —— that right we hold
> By His donation; but man over men
> He made not lord, such title to Himself
> Reserving, human left from human free.

Slavery tyrannically assumes a power which Heaven denied; while under its barbarous necromancy, borrowed from the Source of Evil, a man is changed into a chattel, a person is withered into a thing, a soul is shrunk into merchandise. Say, sir, in your madness, that you own the sun, the stars, the moon; but do not say that you own a man, endowed with a soul that shall live immortal, when sun and moon and stars have passed away.

Secondly. Slavery paints itself again in its complete *abrogation of marriage*, recognized as a sacrament by the church, and recognized as a contract wherever civilization prevails. Under the law of Slavery, no such sacrament is respected, and no such contract can exist. The ties that may be formed between slaves are all subject to the selfish interests or more selfish lust of the master, whose license knows no check. Natural affections, which have come together, are rudely torn asunder; nor is this all. Stripped of every defence, the chastity of a whole race is exposed to violence, while the result is recorded in the tell-tale faces of children, glowing with their master's blood, but doomed for their mother's skin to Slavery, through all descending generations. The Senator from Mississippi [Mr. BROWN] is galled by the comparison between Slavery and Polygamy, and winces. I hail this sensibility as the sign of virtue. Let him reflect, and he will confess that there are many disgusting elements in Slavery, which are not present in Polygamy, while the single disgusting element of Polygamy is more than present in Slavery. By the license of Polygamy, one man may have many wives, all bound to him by the marriage-tie, and in other respects protected by law. By the license of Slavery, a whole race is delivered over to prostitution and concubinage, without the protection of any law. Sir, is not Slavery barbarous?

Thirdly. Slavery paints itself again in its complete *abrogation of the parental relation*, which God in his benevolence has provided for the nurture and education of the human family, and which constitutes an essential part of Civilization itself. And yet, by the law of Slavery — happily beginning to be modified in some places — this relation is set at naught, and in its place is substituted the arbitrary control of the master, at whose mere command little children, such as the Saviour called unto him, though clasped by a mother's arms, may be swept under the hammer of the auctioneer. I do not dwell on this exhibition. Sir, is not Slavery barbarous?

Fourthly. Slavery paints itself again *in closing the gates of knowledge,* which are also the shining gates of civilization. Under its plain unequivocal law, the bondman may, at the unrestrained will of his master, be shut out from all instruction; while in many places, incredible to relate! the law itself, by cumulative provisions, positively forbids that he shall be taught to read. Of course, the slave can not be allowed to read, for his soul would then expand in larger air, while he saw the glory of the North Star, and also the helping truth, that God, who made iron, never made a slave; for he would then become familiar with the Scriptures, with the Decalogue still speaking in the thunders of Sinai; with that ancient text, "He that stealeth a man and selleth him, or if he be found in his hands, he shall surely be put to death;" with that other text, "Masters, give unto your servants that which is just and equal;" with that great story of redemption, when the Lord raised the slave-born Moses to deliver his chosen people from the house of bondage; and with that sublimer story, where the Saviour died a cruel death, that all men, without distinction of race, might be saved — leaving to mankind commandments, which, even without his example, make Slavery impossible. Thus, in order to fasten your manacles upon the slave, you fasten other manacles upon his soul. Sir, is not Slavery barbarous?

Fifthly. Slavery paints itself again *in the appropriation of all the toil* of its victims, excluding them from that property in their own earnings which the law of nature allows, and civilization secures. The painful injustice of this pretension is lost in its meanness. It is robbery and petty larceny, under the garb of law. And even its meanness is lost in the absurdity of its associate pretension, that the African, thus despoiled of all his earnings, is saved from poverty, and that for his own good he must work for his master, and not for himself. Alas! by such a fallacy, is a whole race pauperized! And yet this transaction is not without illustrative example. A solemn poet, whose verse has found wide favor, pictures a creature who,

> ——— With one hand put
> A penny in the urn of poverty,
> And with the other took a shilling out.
> *Pollok's "Course of Time," Book VIII.* 632.

And a celebrated traveller through Russia, more than a generation ago, describes a kindred spirit, who, while on his knees before an altar of the Greek Church, devoutly told his beads with one hand, and with the other deliberately picked the pocket of a fellow-sinner by his side. Not admiring these instances, I can not cease to deplore a system which has much of both, while, under an affectation of charity, it sordidly takes from the slave all the fruits of his bitter sweat, and thus takes from him the mainspring to exertion. Tell me, sir, is not Slavery barbarous?

Such is Slavery in its five special elements of Barbarism, as recognized by law; first, assuming that man can hold property in man; secondly, abrogating the relation of husband and wife; thirdly, abrogating the parental tie; fourthly, closing the gates of knowledge; and fifthly, appropriating the unpaid labor of another. Take away these elements, sometimes called "abuses," and Slavery will cease to exist, for it is these very "abuses" which constitute Slavery. Take away any one of them, and the abolition of Slavery begins. And when I present Slavery for judgment, I mean no slight evil, with regard to which there may be a reasonable difference of opinion, but I mean this five-fold embodiment of "abuse"— this ghastly quincunx of Barbarism — each particular of which, if considered separately, must be denounced at once with all the ardor of an honest soul, while the whole five-fold combination must awake a five-fold denunciation.

But this five-fold combination becomes still more hateful when its *single motive* is considered. The Senator from Mississippi [Mr. DAVIS] says that it is "but a form of civil government for those who are not fit to govern themselves." The Senator is mistaken. It is an outrage where five different pretensions all concur in one single object, looking only to the profit of the master, and constituting its ever-present motive power, which is simply to *compel the labor of fellow-men without wages!*

If the offense of Slavery were less extended; if it were confined to some narrow region; if it had less of grandeur in its proportions; if its victims were counted by tens and hundreds, instead of millions, the five-headed enormity would find little indulgence. All would rise against it, while religion and civilization would lavish their choicest efforts in the general warfare. But what is wrong, when done to one man, can not be right when done to many. If it is wrong thus to degrade a single soul — if it is wrong thus to degrade you, Mr. President — it can not be right to degrade a whole race. And yet this is denied by the barbarous logic of Slavery, which, taking advantage of its own wrong, claims immunity because its usurpation has assumed a front of audacity that can not be safely attacked. Unhappily, there is Barbarism elsewhere in the world; but American Slavery, as defined by existing law, stands forth as the greatest organized Barbarism on which the sun now shines.' It is without a single peer. Its author, after making it, broke the die.

If curiosity carries us to the origin of this law — and here I approach a topic often considered in this Chamber — we shall confess again its Barbarism. It is not derived from the common law, that fountain of Liberty; for this law, while unhappily recognizing a system of servitude known as villeinage, secured to the bondman privileges unknown to the American slave; protected his person against mayhem; protected his wife against rape; gave to his marriage equal validity with the marriage of his master, and surrounded his offspring with generous presumptions of Freedom, unlike that rule of yours by which the servitude of the mother is necessarily stamped upon the child. It is not derived from the Roman law, that fountain of tyranny, for two reasons: first, because this law, in its better days, when its early rigors were spent — like the common law itself — secured to the bondman privileges unknown to the American slave — in certain cases of cruelty, rescued him from his master — prevented the separation of parents and children, also of brothers and sisters — and even protected him in the marriage relation; and secondly, because the Thirteen Colonies

18

were not derived from any of those countries which recognized the Roman law, while this law, even before the discovery of this continent, had lost all living efficacy. It is not derived from the Mohammedan law; for under the mild injunctions of the Koran, a benignant servitude, unlike yours, has prevailed — where the lash is not allowed to lacerate the back of a female; where no knife or branding-iron is employed upon any human being, to mark him as the property of his fellow-man; where the master is expressly enjoined to listen to the desires of his slave for emancipation; and where the blood of the master, mingling with his bond-woman, takes from her the transferable character of a chattel, and confers complete freedom upon their offspring. It is not derived from the Spanish law, for this law contains humane elements unknown to your system, borrowed, perhaps, from the Mohammedan Moors who so long occupied Spain; and besides, our Thirteen Colonies had no umbilical connection with Spain. Nor is it derived from English statutes or American statutes; for we have the positive and repeated averment of the Senator from Virginia, [Mr. MASON,] and also of other Senators, that in not a single State of the Union can any such statutes establishing Slavery be found. From none of these does it come.

No, sir; not from any land of civilization is this Barbarism derived. It comes from Africa, ancient nurse of monsters; from Guinea, Dahomey, and Congo. There is its origin and fountain. This benighted region, we are told by Chief-Justice Marshall in a memorable judgment, (*The Antelope*, 10 Wheaton R. 66,) still asserts a right, discarded by Christendom, to enslave captives taken in war; and this African Barbarism is the beginning of American Slavery. And the Supreme Court of Georgia, a Slave State, has not shrunk from this conclusion. "Licensed to hold slave property," says the Court, "the Georgia planter held the slave as a chattel; either directly from the slave-trader, or from those who held under him, and he from the slave-captor in Africa. The property of the planter in the slave became, thus, the property of the original captor." (*Neal* v. *Farmer*, 9 *Georgia Reports, p.* 555.) It is natural that a right, thus derived in defiance of Christendom, and openly founded on the most vulgar Paganism, should be exercised without any mitigating influence from Christianity; that the master's authority over the person of his slave — over his conjugal relations — over his parental relations — over the employment of his time — over all his acquisitions, should be recognized, while no generous presumption inclines to Freedom, and the womb of the bond-woman can deliver only a slave.

From its home in Africa, where it is sustained by immemorial usage, this Barbarism, thus derived and thus developed, traversed the ocean to American soil. It entered on board that fatal slave-ship "built in the eclipse, and rigged with curses dark," which in 1620 landed its cruel cargo at Jamestown, in Virginia, and it has boldly taken its place in every succeeding slave-ship from that early day till now—helping to pack the human freight, regardless of human agony; surviving the torments of the middle passage; surviving its countless victims plunged beneath the waves; and it has left the slave-ship only to travel inseparable from the slave in his various doom, sanctioning by its barbarous code every outrage, whether of mayhem or robbery, of lash or lust, and fastening itself upon his offspring to the remotest generation. Thus are the barbarous prerogatives of barbarous half-naked African chiefs perpetuated in American Slave-masters, while the Senator from Virginia, [Mr. MASON,] perhaps unconscious of their origin— perhaps desirous to secure for them the appearance of a less barbarous pedigree—tricks them out with a phrase of the Roman law, discarded by the common law, *partus sequitur ventrem*, which simply renders into ancient Latin an existing rule of African Barbarism, recognized as an existing rule of American Slavery.

Such is the plain juridical origin of the American slave code, which is now vaunted as a badge of Civilization. But all law, whatever may be its juridical origin, whether English or Mohammedan, Roman or African, may be traced to other and ampler influences in nature, sometimes of Right, and sometimes of Wrong. Surely the law which blasted the slave-trade as piracy punishable with death had a different inspiration from that other law, which secured immunity for the slave-trade throughout an immense territory, and invested its supporters with political power. As there is a higher law above, so there is a lower law below, and each is felt in human affairs.

Thus far we have seen Slavery only in its pretended law,

20

and in the origin of that law. And here I might stop without proceeding in this argument, for on the letter of the law alone Slavery must be condemned. But the tree is known by its fruits, and these I now shall exhibit—and this brings me to the second stage of the argument.

(2.) In considering the *practical results of Slavery*, the materials are so obvious and diversified that my chief care will be to abridge and reject; and here I shall put the Slave States and Free States face to face, showing at each point the blasting influence of Slavery.

The States where this Barbarism now exists excel the Free States in all natural advantages. Their territory is more extensive, stretching over 851,448 square miles, while the Free States, including California, embrace only 612,597 square miles. Here is a difference of more than 238,000 square miles in favor of the Slave States, showing that Freedom starts, in this great controversy, with a field more than a quarter less than that of Slavery. In happiness of climate, adapted to productions of special value; in exhaustless motive power distributed throughout its space; in natural highways, by more than fifty navigable rivers, never closed by the rigors of winter; and in a stretch of coast along ocean and gulf, indented by hospitable harbors— the whole presenting incomparable advantages for that true civilization, where agriculture, manufactures and commerce, both domestic and foreign, blend—in all these respects the Slave States excel the Free States, whose climate is often churlish, whose motive power is less various, whose navigable rivers are fewer and often sealed by ice, and whose coast, while less in extent and with fewer harbors, is often perilous from storm and cold.

But Slavery plays the part of a Harpy, and defiles the choicest banquet. See what it does with this territory, thus spacious and fair.

An important indication of prosperity is to be found in the growth of *population*. In this respect the two regions started equal. In 1790, at the first census under the Constitution, the population of the present Slave States was 1,961,372, of the present Free States 1,968,455, showing a difference of only 7083 in favor of the Free States. This difference, at first merely nominal, has been constantly increasing since, showing itself more strongly in each decennial census, until in 1850, the population of the Slave States, swollen by the annexation of three foreign Territories, Louisiana, Florida, and Texas, was only 9,612,769, while that of the Free States, without any such annexations, reached 13,434,922, showing a difference of 3,822,153 in favor of Freedom. But this difference becomes still more remarkable, if we confine our inquiries to the white population, which at this period was only 6,184,477 in the Slave States, while it was 13,238,670 in the Free States, showing a difference of more than 7,054,193, in favor of Freedom, and showing that the white population of the Free States had not only doubled, but commenced to triple that of the Slave States, although occupying a smaller territory. The comparative sparseness of the two populations furnishes another illustration. In the Slave States the average number of inhabitants to a square mile was 11.28, while in the Free States it was 21.93, or almost two to one in favor of Freedom.

These results are general; but if we take any particular Slave State, and compare it with a Free State, we shall find the same constant evidence for Freedom. Take Virginia, with a territory of 61,352 miles, and New-York, with a territory of 47,000, or over 14,000 square miles less than her sister State. New-York has one sea-port, Virginia some three or four; New-York has one noble river, Virginia has several; New-York for 400 miles runs along the frozen line of Canada; Virginia basks in a climate of constant felicity. But Freedom is better than climate, rivers, or sea-port!

In 1790 the population of Virginia was 748,308, and in 1850 it was 1,421,661. In 1790, the population of New-York was 340,120, and in 1850 it was 3,097,394; that of Virginia had not doubled in sixty years, while that of New-York had multiplied more than nine-fold. A similar comparison may be made between Kentucky, with 37,680 square miles, admitted into the Union as long ago as 1790, and Ohio, with 39,964 square miles, admitted into the Union in 1802. In 1850, the Slave State had a population of only 982,405, while Ohio had a population of 1,980,329, showing a difference of nearly a million in favor of Freedom.

As in population, so also in the *value of property, real and personal,* do the Free States excel the Slave States. According

22

to the census of 1850, the value of property in the Free States was $4,107,162,198, while in the Slave States it was $2,936,090,-737; or, if we deduct the asserted property in human flesh, only $1,655,945,137—showing an enormous difference of billions in favor of Freedom. In the Free States the valuation per acre was $10.47, in the Slave States only $3.04. This disproportion was still greater in 1855, according to the report of the Secretary of the Treasury, when the valuation of the Free States was $5,770,194,680; or $14.72 per acre; and of the Slave States, $3,977,353,946, or if we deduct the asserted property in human flesh, $2,505,186,346, or $4.59 per acre. Thus in five years from 1850, the valuation of property in the Free States received an increase of more than the whole accumulated valuation of the Slave States at that time.

Looking at details, we find the same disproportions. Arkansas and Michigan, equal in territory, were admitted into the Union in the same year; and yet in 1855, the whole valuation of Arkansas, including its asserted property in human flesh, was only $64,240,726, while that of Michigan, without a single slave, was $116,593,580. The whole accumulated valuation of all the Slave States, deducting the asserted property in human flesh, in 1850, was only $1,655,945,137; but the valuation of New-York alone, in 1855, reached the nearly equal sum of $1,401,285,279. The valuation of Virginia, North and South-Carolina, Georgia, Florida, and Texas, all together, in 1850, deducting human flesh, was $573,332,860, or simply $1.81 per acre—being less than that of Massachusetts alone, which was $573,342,286, or $114.85 per acre.

The Slave States boast of *agriculture*; but here again, notwithstanding their superior natural advantages, they must yield to the Free States at every point, in the number of farms and plantations, in the number of acres of improved lands, in the cash value of farms, in the average value per acre, and in the value of farming implements and machinery. Here is a short table:

Free States.—Number of farms, 877,736; acres of improved land, 57,688,040; cash value of farms, $2,143,344,437; average value per acre, $19.83; value of farming implements, $85,736,-658.

Slave States.—Number of farms, 564,203; acres of improved

land, 54,970,427; cash value of farms, $1,117,649,649; average value per acre, $6.18; value of farming implements $65,345,625.

Such is the mighty contrast. But it does not stop here. Careful tables place the agricultural products of the Free States, for the year ending June, 1850, at $858,634,334, while those of the Slave States were $631,277,417; the product per acre in the Free States at $7.94, and the product per acre in the Slave States at $3.49; and the average product of each agriculturist in the Free States at $342, and in the Slave States at $171. Thus the Free States, with a smaller population engaged in agriculture than the Slave States, with smaller territory, show an annual sum total of agricultural products surpassing those of the Slave States by two hundred and twenty-seven millions of dollars, while twice as much is produced on an acre, and more than twice as much is produced by each agriculturist. The monopoly of cotton, rice, and cane-sugar, with a climate granting two and sometimes three crops in the year, are thus impotent in the competition with Freedom.

In *manufactures*, the failure of the Slave States is greater still. It appears at all points, in the capital employed, in the value of the raw material, in the annual wages, and in the annual product. A short table will show the contrast:

Free States.—Capital, $430,240,051; value of raw material, $465,844,092; annual wages, $195,976,453; annual product, $842,586,058.

Slave States.—Capital, $95,029,879; value of raw material, $86,190,639; annual wages, $33,257,360; annual product, $165,413,027.

This might be illustrated by details with regard to different manufactures — whether of shoes, cotton, woollen, pig-iron, wrought-iron, and iron castings — all showing the contrast. It might also be illustrated by a comparison between different States; showing, for instance, that the manufactures of Massachusetts, during the last year, exceeded those of all the Slave States combined.

In *commerce*, the failure of the Slave States is on yet a larger scale. Under this head, the census does not supply proper statistics, and we are left, therefore, to approximations from other quarters; but these are enough for our purpose. It appears that, of the products which enter into commerce, the Free

States had an amount valued at $1,377,199,968 ; the Slave States an amount valued only at $410,754,992 ; that of the persons engaged in trade, the Free States had 136,856, and the Slave States, 52,622 ; and that of the tonnage employed, the Free States had 2,790,195 tons, and the Slave States, only 726,285. This was in 1850. But in 1855 the disproportion was still greater, the Free States having 4,252,615 tons, and the Slave States 855,517 tons, being a difference of five to one ; and the tonnage of Massachusetts alone being 970,727 tons, an amount larger than that of all the Slave States. The tonnage built during this year by the Free States was 528,844 tons ; by the Slaves States, 52,959 tons. Maine alone built 215,905 tons, or more than four times the whole built in the Slave States.

The foreign commerce, as indicated by the exports and imports in 1855, of the Free States, was $404,368,503 ; of the Slave States, $132,067,216. The exports of the Free States were $167,520,693 ; of the Slave States, including the vaunted cotton crop, $132,007,216. The imports of the Free States were $236,847,810 ; of the Slave States, $24,586,528. The foreign commerce of New-York alone was more than twice as large as that of all the Slave States ; her imports were larger, and her exports were larger also. Add to this testimony of figures the testimony of a Virginian, Mr. Loudon, in a letter written just before the sitting of a Southern Commercial Convention. Thus he complains and testifies :

"There are not half a dozen vessels engaged in our own trade that are owned in Virginia ; and I have been unable to find a vessel at Liverpool loading for Virginia within three years, during the height of our busy season."

Railroads and canals are the avenues of commerce ; and here again the Free States excel. Of railroads in operation in 1854, there were 13,105 miles in the Free States, and 4212 in the Slave States. Of canals there were 3,682 miles in the Free States, and 1116 in the Slave States.

The *Post-Office*, which is not only the agent of commerce, but of civilization, joins in the uniform testimony. According to the tables for 1859, the postage collected in the Free States was $5,532,999, and the expense of carrying the mails $6,748,189, leaving a deficit of $1,215,189. In the Slave States the amount collected was only $1,988,050, and the expense of carrying the mails $6,016,612, leaving the enormous deficit of

$4,028,568; the difference between the two deficits being $2,-813,372. The Slave States did not pay one third of the expense of transporting their mails; and not a single Slave State paid for the transportation of its mails; not even the small State of Delaware. Massachusetts, besides paying for hers, had a surplus larger than the whole amount collected in South-Carolina.

According to the census of 1850, the value of *churches* in the Free States was $67,773,477; in the Slave States, $21,674,581.

The *voluntary charity* contributed in 1855, for certain leading purposes of Christian benevolence, was, in the Free States, $953,813; for the same purposes, in the Slave States, $194,784. For the Bible cause, the Free States contributed $319,667; the Slave States, $68,125. For the missionary cause, the first contributed $319,667; and the second, $101,934. For the Tract Society, the first contributed $131,972; and the second, $24,-725. The amount contributed in Massachusetts for the support of missions was greater than that contributed by all the Slave States, and more than eight times that contributed by South-Carolina.

Nor have the Free States been backward in charity, when the Slave States have been smitten. The records of Massachusetts show that as long ago as 1781, at the beginning of the Government, there was an extensive contribution throughout the Commonwealth, under the particular direction of that eminent patriot, Samuel Adams, for the relief of inhabitants of South-Carolina and Georgia. In 1855, we were saddened by the prevalence of yellow fever in Portsmouth, Virginia; and now, from a report of the relief committee of that place, we learn that the amount of charity contributed by the Slave States, exclusive of Virginia, the afflicted State, was $12,182; and, including Virginia, it was $33,398; while $42,547 were contributed by the Free States.

In all this array we see the fatal influence of Slavery, but its Barbarism is yet more conspicuous when we consider its *Educational Establishments*, and the unhappy results, which naturally ensue from their imperfect character.

Of *colleges*, in 1856, the Free States had 61, and the Slave States 59; but the comparative efficacy of the institutions, which assume this name, may be measured by certain facts.

26

The number of graduates in the Free States was 47,752, in the Slave States, 19,648; the number of ministers educated in Slave colleges was 747, in the Free colleges, 10,702; and the number of volumes in the libraries of Slave colleges, 308,011; in the libraries of the Free colleges, 667,227. If the materials were at hand for a comparison between these colleges, in buildings, cabinets, and scientific apparatus, or in the standard of scholarship, the difference would be still more apparent.

Of *professional schools*, teaching law, medicine, and theology, the Free States had 65, with 269 professors, 4426 students, and 175,951 volumes in their libraries; while the Slave States had only 32 professional schools, with 122 professors, 1807 students, and 30,796 volumes in their libraries. The whole number educated at these institutions in the Free States was 23,513, in the Slave States, 3812. Of these, the largest number in the Slave States study law, next medicine, and lastly theology. According to the census, there are only 808 in the Slave theological schools, and 747 studying for the ministry in the Slave colleges; and this is all the record we have of the education of the Slave clergy.

Of *academies and private schools*, in 1850, the Free States, notwithstanding their multitudinous public schools, had 3197, with 7175 teachers, 154,893 pupils, and an annual income of $2,457,372; the Slave States had 2797 academies and private schools, with 4913 teachers, 104,976 pupils, and an annual income of $2,079,724. In the absence of public schools, to a large extent, where Slavery exists, the dependence must be chiefly upon private schools; and yet even in these the Slave States fall below the Free States, whether we consider the number of pupils, the number of teachers, or the amount paid for their support.

In *public schools*, open to all, alike the poor and the rich, the eminence of the Free States is complete. Here the figures show a difference as wide as that between Freedom and Slavery. Their number in the Free States is 62,433, with 72,621 teachers, and with 2,769,901 pupils, supported by an annual expense of $6,780,337. Their number in the Slave States is 18,507, with 19,307 teachers, and with 581,861 pupils, supported by an annual expense of $2,719,534. This difference may be illustrated by details. Virginia, an old State, and more than a third larger than Ohio, has 67,353 pupils in her public schools, while the latter State has 484,153. Arkansas, equal in age and size with Michigan, has only 8493 pupils at her public schools, while the latter State has 110,455. South-Carolina, three times as large as Massachusetts, has 17,838 pupils at public school, while the latter State has 176,475. South-Carolina spends, for this purpose, annually, $200,600; Massachusetts, $1,006,795. Baltimore, with a population of 169,012, on the northern verge of Slavery, has school buildings valued at $105,729; those of Boston are valued at $729,502. Boston, with a population smaller than that of Baltimore, has 203 public schools, with 353 teachers, and 21,678 pupils, supported at an annual expense of $237,000; Baltimore has only 36 public schools, with 138 teachers, and 8011 pupils, supported at an annual expense of $32,423. But even these figures do not disclose the whole difference; for there exist in the Free States teachers' institutes, normal schools, lyceums, and public courses of lectures, which are unknown in the region of Slavery. These advantages are enjoyed also by the children of colored persons; and here is a comparison which shows the degradation of the Slave States. It is their habit particularly to deride free colored persons. See, now, with what cause. The number of colored persons in the Free States is 196,016, of whom 22,043, or more than one ninth, attend school, which is a larger proportion than is supplied by the whites of the Slave States. In Massachusetts there are 9064 colored persons, of whom 1439, or nearly one sixth, attend school, which is a much larger proportion than is supplied by the whites of South-Carolina.

Among educational establishments are *public libraries;* and here, again, the Free States have their customary eminence, whether we consider libraries strictly called public, or libraries of the common-school, of the Sunday-school, of the college, and of the church. Here the disclosures are startling. The number of libraries in the Free States is 14,911, and the sum total of volumes is 3,888,234; the number of libraries in the Slave States is 695, and the sum total of volumes is 649,577; showing an excess for Freedom of more than fourteen thousand libraries, and more than three millions of volumes. In the Free States, the common-school libraries are 11,881, and contain 1,5s9,683 volumes; in the Slave States they are 186, and contain 57,721 volumes. In the Free States the Sunday-school libraries are 1713, and contain 478,858 volumes; in the Slave States they are 275, and contain 63,463 volumes. In the Free States the college libraries are 132, and contain 660,573 volumes; in the Slave States they are 79, and contain 249,248 volumes. In the Free States the church libraries are 109, and contain 52,723 volumes; in the Slave States they are 21, and contain 5627 volumes. In the Free States the libraries strictly called public, and not included under the heads already enumerated, are 1058, and contain 1,106,397 volumes; those of the Slave States are 152, and contain 273,518 volumes.

Turn these figures over, look at them in any light, and the conclusion will be irresistible for Freedom. The college libraries alone of the Free States are greater than all the libraries of Slavery. So, also, are the libraries of Massachusetts alone greater than all the libraries of Slavery; and the common-school libraries alone of New-York are more than twice as large as all the libraries of Slavery. Michigan has 107,943 volumes in her libraries; Arkansas has 420.

Among educational establishments, one of the most efficient is the *Press;* and here again all things testify for Freedom. The Free States excel in the number of newspapers and periodicals published, whether daily, semi-weekly, weekly, semi-monthly, monthly, or quarterly; and whatever their character, whether literary, neutral, political, religious, or scientific. The whole aggregate circulation in the Free States is 334,146,281; in the Slave States, 81,038,693. In Free Michigan, 3,247,736; in Slave Arkansas, 377,000. In Free Ohio, 30,473,407; in Slave Kentucky, 6,582,838. In Slave South-Carolina, 7,145,- 930; in Free Massachusetts, 64,820,564—a larger number than in the ten Slave States, Maryland, Virginia, North-Carolina, South-Carolina, Georgia, Alabama, Mississippi, Florida, Louisiana, and Texas, combined. This enormous disproportion in the aggregate is also preserved in the details. In the Slave States, political newspapers find more favor than any others; but even of these they publish only 47,243,209 copies, while the Free States publish 163,583,668. Of neutral newspapers, the Slave States publish 8,812,620; the Free States, 79,156,738. Of religious newspapers, the Slave States publish 4,364,832; the Free States, 29,280,652. Of literary journals, the Slave

States publish 20,245,360; the Free States, 57,478,768. And of scientific journals, the Slave States publish 372,672; the Free States, 4,521,260. Of these latter, the number of copies published in Massachusetts alone is 2,033,260—more than five times the number in the whole land of Slavery. Thus, in contributions to science, literature, religion, and even politics, as attested by the activity of the periodical press, do the Slave States miserably fail, while darkness gathers over them. And this seems to be increasing with time. According to the census of 1810, the disproportion in this respect between the two regions was only as two to one. It is now more than five to one, and is still going on.

The same disproportion appears with regard to persons connected with the Press. In the Free States, the number of *printers* was 11,822, of whom 1229 were in Massachusetts; in the Slave States there were 2895, of whom South-Carolina had only 141. In the Free States, the number of *publishers* was 331; in the Slave States, 24. Of these, Massachusetts had 59, or more than twice as many as all the Slave States; while South-Carolina had none. In the Free States, the *authors* were 73; in the Slave States, 9—of whom Massachusetts had 17, and South-Carolina 2. These suggestive illustrations are all derived from the last official census. But if we go to other sources, the contrast is still the same. Of the authors mentioned in Duyckink's Cyclopedia of American Literature, 403 are of the Free States, and only 87 of the Slave States. Of the poets mentioned in Griswold's Poets and Poetry of America, 123 are of the Free States, and only 17 of the Slave States. Of the poets, whose place of birth appears in Reed's Female Poets of America, 73 are of the Free States, and only 11 of the Slave States. And if we try authors by weight or quality, it is the same as when we try them by numbers. Out of the Free States have come all whose works have taken a place in the permanent literature of the country—Irving, Prescott, Sparks, Bancroft, Emerson, Motley, Hildreth, and Hawthorne; also, Bryant, Longfellow, Dana, Halleck, Whittier, and Lowell—and I might add indefinitely to the list. But what name from the Slave States could find a place there?

A similar disproportion appears in the number of *Patents*, attesting the inventive industry of the contrasted regions, issued during the last three years, 1857, 1858, and 1859. In the Free States there were 9560; in the Slave States, 1449—making a difference of 8111 in favor of Freedom. The number in Free Massachusetts was 972; in Slave South-Carolina, 39. The number in Free Connecticut, small in territory and population, was 628; in Slave Virginia, large in territory and population, 184.

From all these things we might infer the *ignorance* prevalent in the Slave States; but this shows itself in specific results of a deplorable character, authenticated by the official census. It appears that in the Slave States there were 493,026 native white persons over twenty years of age who can not read and write, while in the Free States, with double the white population, there were but 248,725 native whites over twenty years of age in this unhappy predicament. In the Slave States the proportion was 1 to 12; in the Free States it was 1 to 53. The number in Free Massachusetts, with a population of nearly a million, was 1005, or 1 in 517; the number in Slave South-Carolina, with a population under three hundred thousand, was 15,580, or 1 in 7. The number in Free Connecticut was 1 in 277; in Slave Virginia, 1 in 5; in Free New-Hampshire, 1 in 201, and in Slave North-Carolina, 1 in 3.

Before closing this picture of Slavery, where the dismal colors all come from official figures, there are two other aspects in which for a moment it may be regarded:

1. The first is the influence which it has on *emigration*. It is stated in the official compendium of the census, (page 115,) that those persons living in Slave States who are natives of Free States are more numerous than those living in Free States who are natives of Slaves States. This is an egregious error. Just the contrary is true. The census of 1850 found 609,371 in the Free States who were born in the Slave States, while only 206,-638 born in the Free States were in the Slave States. And since the white population of the Free States is double that of the Slave States, it appears that the proportion of whites moving from Slavery is six times greater than that of whites moving into Slavery. In this simple fact is disclosed something of the aversion to Slavery which is aroused even in the Slave States.

2. The second aspect is furnished by the character of the region on the border-line between Freedom and Slavery. In gen-

eral, the value of lands in Slave States adjoining Freedom is advanced, while the value of corresponding lands in Free States is diminished. The effects of Freedom and Slavery are reciprocal. Slavery is a bad neighbor. Freedom is a good neighbor. In Virginia, lands naturally poor are, by their nearness to Freedom, worth $12.98 an acre, while richer lands in other parts of the State are worth only $8.42. In Illinois, lands bordering upon Slavery are worth only $4.54 an acre, while other lands in Illinois are worth $8.05. As in the value of lands so in all other influences is Slavery felt for evil, and Freedom felt for good; and thus is it clearly shown to be for the interest of the Slave States to be surrounded by a circle of Free States.

Thus, at every point is the character of Slavery more and more manifest, rising and dilating into an overshadowing Barbarism, darkening the whole land. Through its influence, population, values of all kinds, manufactures, commerce, railroads, canals, charities, the post-office, colleges, professional schools, academies, public schools, newspapers, periodicals, books, authorship, inventions, are all stunted, and, under a Government which professes to be founded on the intelligence of the people, one in twelve of the white adults in the region of Slavery is officially reported as unable to read and write. Never was the saying of Montesquieu more triumphantly verified, that countries are not cultivated by reason of their fertility, but by reason of their liberty. To this truth the Slave States constantly testify by every possible voice. Liberty is the powerful agent which drives the plow, the spindle, and the keel; which opens avenues of all kinds; which inspires charity; which awakens a love of knowledge, and supplies the means of gratifying it. Liberty is the first of schoolmasters.

Unerring and passionless figures thus far have been our witnesses. But their testimony will be enhanced by a final glance at the *geographical character* of the Slave States; and here there is a singular and instructive parallel.

Jefferson described Virginia as fast sinking to be "the Barbary of the Union"—meaning, of course, the Barbary of his day, which had not yet turned against Slavery. In this allusion he was wiser than he knew. Though on different sides of the Atlantic and on different continents, our Slave States and the original Barbary States occupy nearly the same parallels of latitude;

occupy nearly the same extent of longitude; embrace nearly the same number of square miles; enjoy kindred advantages of climate, being equally removed from the cold of the North and the burning heat of the tropics; and also enjoy kindred boundaries of land and water, with kindred advantages of ocean and sea, with this difference, that the boundaries of the two regions are precisely reversed, so that where is land in one case is water in the other, while in both cases there is the same extent of ocean and the same extent of sea. Nor is this all. Algiers, for a long time the most obnoxious place in the Barbary States of Africa, once branded by an indignant chronicler as "the wall of the barbarian world," is situated near the parallel of 36° 30′ north latitude, being the line of the Missouri compromise, which once marked the "wall" of Slavery in our country west of the Mississippi, while Morocco, the chief present seat of Slavery in the African Barbary, is on the parallel of Charleston. There are no two spaces on the surface of the globe, equal in extent, (and an examination of the map will verify what I am about to state,) which present so many distinctive features of resemblance; whether we consider the common parallels of latitude on which they lie, the common nature of their boundaries, their common productions, their common climate, or the common Barbarism which sought shelter in both. I do not stop to inquire why Slavery—banished at last from Europe, banished also from that part of this hemisphere which corresponds in latitude to Europe —should have intrenched itself in both hemispheres between the same parallels of latitude, so that Virginia, Carolina, Mississippi, and Missouri, should be the American complement to Morocco, Algiers, Tripoli, and Tunis. But there is one important point in the parallel which remains to be fulfilled. The barbarous Emperor of Morocco, in the words of a Treaty, has expressed his desire that Slavery might pass from the memory of men, while Algiers, Tripoli, and Tunis, after cherishing Slavery with a tenacity equaled only by the tenacity of South-Carolina, have successively renounced it and delivered it over to the indignation of mankind. In following this example the parallel will be complete, and our Barbary will become the complement in Freedom to the African Barbary, as it has already been its complement in Slavery, and is unquestionably its complement in geographical character.

II. From the consideration of Slavery in its practical results, illustrated by the contrast between the Free States and Slave States, I pass now to another stage of the argument, and proceed to exhibit Slavery in its influence on the CHARACTER OF SLAVE-MASTERS. Nothing could I undertake more painful, and yet there is nothing which is more essential to the discussion, especially in response to the pretensions of Senators on this floor, nor is there any point on which the evidence is more complete.

It is in the Character of Slavery itself that we are to find the Character of Slave-masters; but I need not go back to the golden lips of Chrysostom, to learn that "Slavery is the fruit of covetousness, of extravagance, of insatiable greediness;" for we have already seen that this five-fold enormity is inspired by the single idea of *compelling men to work without wages.* This spirit must naturally appear in the Slave-master. But the eloquent Christian Saint did not disclose the whole truth. Slavery is founded on violence, as we have already too clearly seen; of course it can be sustained only by kindred violence, sometimes against the defenseless slave, sometimes against the freeman whose indignation is aroused at the outrage. It is founded on brutal and vulgar pretensions, as we have already too clearly seen; of course it can be sustained only by kindred brutality and vulgarity. The denial of all rights in the slave can be sustained only by a disregard of other rights, common to the whole community, whether of the person, of the press, or of speech. Where this exists there can be but one supreme law, to which all other laws, legislative or social, are subordinate, and this is the pretended law of Slavery. All these things must be manifest in Slave-masters, and yet, unconscious of their true condition, they make boasts which reveal still further the unhappy influence. Barbarous standards of conduct are unblushingly avowed. The swagger of a bully is called chivalry; a swiftness to quarrel is called courage; the bludgeon is adopted as the substitute for argument; and assassination is lifted to be one of the Fine Arts. Long ago it was fixed certain that the day which made man a slave "took half his worth away"— words from the ancient harp of Homer, resounding through long generations. Nothing here is said of the human being at the other end of the chain. To aver that, on this

34

same day, all his worth is taken away, might seem inconsistent with exceptions which we gladly recognize; but alas! it is too clear, both from reason and from evidence, that, bad as Slavery is for the Slave, it is worse for the Master.

In making this exposure I am fortified, at the outset, by two classes of authorities, whose testimony it will be difficult to question; the first is American, and founded on personal experience; the second is philosophical, and founded on everlasting truth.

First, *American Authority*; and here I adduce words often quoted, which dropped from the lips of Slave-masters in those better days, when, seeing the wrong of Slavery, they escaped from its injurious influence. Of these, none expressed themselves with more vigor than Colonel Mason, a Slave-master from Virginia, in debate on the adoption of the National Constitution. These are his words:

"Slavery discourages arts and manufactures. The poor despise labor when performed by slaves. They prevent the emigration of whites, who really enrich and strengthen a country. *They produce the most pernicious effect on manners.* EVERY MASTER OF SLAVES IS BORN A PETTY TYRANT. They bring the judgment of Heaven on a country."

Thus, with a few touches, does this Slave-master portray his class, putting them in that hateful list which, according to every principle of liberty, must be resisted so long as we obey God. And this same testimony also found expression from the fiery soul of Jefferson. Here are some of his words:

"There must be an unhappy influence on the manners of our people, produced by the existence of Slavery among us. The whole commerce between master and slave is a perpetual exercise of the most boisterous passions, THE MOST UNREMITTING DESPOTISM on the one part, and degrading submissions on the other; our children see this, and learn to imitate it. . . . *The man must be a prodigy who can retain his manners and morals undepraved by such circumstances.* And with what execration should the statesman be loaded, who, permitting one half the citizens thus to trample on the rights of the other, *transforms those into despots*, and these into enemies, destroys the morals of the one part, and the *amor patriæ* of the other! . . . With the morals of the people, their industry also is destroyed."

Next comes the *Philosophic Authority*; and here the language which I quote may be less familiar, but it is hardly less commanding. Among names of such weight I shall not discriminate, but shall simply follow the order of time in which they appeared. First is John Locke, the great author of the English system of Intellectual Philosophy, who, though once unhappily conceding indulgence to American Slavery, in another place describes it in words which every Slave-master should know, as—

"The state of war continued between a lawful conqueror and his captive. . . . So opposite to the generous temper and courage of our nation, that *'tis hardly to be conceived that an Englishman, MUCH LESS A GENTLEMAN, should plead for it.*"

Then comes Adam Smith, the founder of the science of Political Economy, who, in his work on Morals, thus utters himself:

"There is not a negro from the coast of Africa who does not possess a degree of magnanimity which the soul of his sordid master is too often scarce capable of conceiving. Fortune never exerted more cruelly her empire over mankind, than when she subjected these nations of heroes to the refuse of jails of Europe, to wretches who possess the virtues neither of the countries which they come from, nor of those which they go to, *and whose levity, brutality, and baseness, so justly expose them to the contempt of the vanquished.*"—*Theory of Moral Sentiments, Part V. Chapter 2.*

This judgment, pronounced just a century ago, was repelled by the Slave-masters of Virginia in a feeble publication, which attests at least their own consciousness that they were the criminals arraigned by the distinguished philosopher. This was soon followed by the testimony of the great English moralist, Dr. Johnson, who, in a letter to a friend, thus shows his opinion of Slave-masters:

"To omit for a year, or for a day, the most efficacious method of advancing Christianity, in compliance with any purposes, that terminate on this side of the grave, is a crime of which I know not that the world has had an example, except in the practice of *the planters of America, a race of mortals whom, I suppose, no other man wishes to resemble.*"—*Letter to William Drummond, 13th August, 1766. (Boswell's Life of Johnson, by Croker.)*

With such authorities, American and Philosophic, I need not hesitate in this ungracious task; but Truth, which is mightier than Mason and Jefferson, than John Locke, Adam Smith, and Samuel Johnson, marshals the evidence in unbroken succession.

Proceeding with this argument, which broadens as we advance, we shall see Slave-masters (1) in the Law of Slavery, (2) in their relations with Slaves, (3) in their relations with each other and with Society, and (4) in that unconsciousness which renders them insensible to their true character.

(1.) As in considering the Character of Slavery, so in considering the Character of Slave-masters, we must begin with the *Law of Slavery,* which, as their work, testifies against them. In the face of such an unutterable abomination, where impiety, cruelty, brutality and robbery, all strive for mastery, it is in vain to assert the humanity or refinement of its authors. Full well I know that the conscience which speaks so powerfully to the solitary soul, is often silent in the corporate body, and that in all ages and countries, numbers, when gathered in communities and States, have sanctioned acts from which the individual revolts. And yet I know no surer way of judging a people than by its laws, especially where those laws have been long continued and openly maintained.

Whatever may be the eminence of individual virtue — and I would not so far disparage humanity as to suppose that the offenses which may be general where Slavery exists are universal — it is not reasonable or logical to infer that the masses of Slave-masters are better than the Law of Slavery. And since the Law itself degrades the slave to be a chattel, and submits him to their irresponsible control — with power to bind and to scourge; to usurp the fruits of another's labor; to pollute the body; and to outrage all ties of family, making marriage impossible — we must conclude that such enormities are sanctioned by Slave-masters; while the exclusion of testimony, and prohibition of instruction — by supplementary law — complete the evidence of their complicity. And this conclusion must stand unquestioned, just so long as the Law of Slavery exists unrepealed. Cease, then, to blazon the humanity of Slave-masters. Tell me not of the lenity with which this cruel Code is tempered to its unhappy subjects. Tell me not of the sympathy which overflows from the mansion of the master to the cabin of the slave. In vain you assert such "happy accidents." In vain you show that there are individuals who do not exert the wickedness of the law. The Barbarism still endures, solemnly, legislatively, judicially attested in the very SLAVE CODE, and proclaims constantly the character of its authors. And this is the first article in the evidence against Slave-masters.

(2.) I am next brought to *Slave-masters in their relations with Slaves;* and here the argument is founded upon facts, and upon presumptions irresistible as facts. Only lately has inquiry burst into that gloomy world of bondage, and disclosed its secrets. But enough is already known to arouse the indignant condemnation of mankind. For instance, here is a simple advertisement — one of thousands — from the *Georgia Messenger:*

"RUN AWAY — My man Fountain; has holes in his ears, a scar on the right side of his forehead; has been shot in the hind parts of his legs; is marked on his back with the whip. Apply to Robert Beasley, Macon, Ga."

Holes in the ears; scar on the forehead; shot in the legs, and marks of the lash on the back! Such are the tokens by which a Slave-master proposes to identify his slave.

And here is another advertisement, revealing Slave-masters in a different light. It is from the *National Intelligencer*, published at the Capital; and I confess the pain with which I cite such an indecency in a journal of such respectability. Of course, it appeared without the knowledge of the editors; but it is none the less an illustrative example:

"FOR SALE.—An accomplished and handsome lady's maid. She is just sixteen years of age; was raised in a genteel family in Maryland; and is now proposed to be sold, not for any fault, but simply because the owner has no further use for her. A note directed to C. D., Gadsby's Hotel, will receive prompt attention."

A sated libertine, in a land where vice is legalized, could not expose his victim with apter words.

These two instances will illustrate a class.

In the recent work of Mr. Olmsted, a close observer and traveler in the Slave States, which abounds in pictures of Slavery, expressed with caution and evident regard to truth, will be found still another, where a Slave-master thus frankly confesses his experience:

" ' I can tell you how you can break a nigger of running away, certain,' said the Slave-master. 'There was an old fellow I used to know in Georgia, that always cured his so. If a nigger ran away, when he caught him, he would bind his knee over a log, and fasten him so he couldn't stir; then he'd take a pair of pincers, and pull one of his toe-nails out by the roots; and tell him, that if he ever run away again, he would pull out two of them; and if he run away again after that, he told him he'd pull out four of them, and so on, doubling each time. He never had to do it more than twice; it always cured them.' "—*Olmsted's Texas Journey*, 105.

Like this story, which is from the lips of a Slave-master, is another, where the master, angry because his slave had sought to regain his God-given liberty, deliberately cut the tendons of his heel, thus horribly maiming him for life!

It is in vain that these instances are denied. Their accumulating number, authenticated in every possible manner, by the press, by a cloud of witnesses, and by the confession of Slave-masters, stares us constantly in the face.

And here we are brought again to the slave code, under the shelter of which these and worse things may be done with complete impunity. Listen to the remarkable words of Chief

Justice Ruffin, of North-Carolina, who, in a solemn decision, thus portrays, affirms, and deplores this terrible latitude :

"'The obedience of the slave,' he says, 'is the consequence only of *uncontrolled authority over the body.* . . . *The power of the master must be absolute, to render the submission of the slave perfect.* I must freely confess my sense of the harshness of this proposition. I feel it as deeply as any man can. And as a principle of moral right, every person in his retirement must repudiate it. But in the actual condition of things, it must be so. There is no remedy. *This discipline belongs to the state of Slavery.* It is inherent in the relation of master and slave.' "—*The State v. Mann, 2 Devereaux R.,* 292.

And this same terrible latitude has been thus expounded in a recent judicial decision of Virginia :

"It is the policy of the law in respect to the relation of master and slave, and for the sake of securing proper subordination and obedience on the part of the slave, *to protect the master from prosecution, even if the whipping and punishment be malicious, cruel, and excessive.*"—*Santher v. Cwelt, 7 Grattan,* 673.

Can Barbarism further go ? Here is an irresponsible power, rendered more irresponsible still by the seclusion of the plantation, and absolutely fortified by the supplementary law excluding the testimony of slaves. That under its shelter enormities should occur, stranger than fiction, too terrible for imagination, and surpassing any individual experience, is simply according to the course of nature and the course of history. The visitation of the abbeys in England disclosed vice and disorder in startling forms, cloaked by the irresponsible privacy of monastic life. A similar visitation of plantations would disclose more fearful results, cloaked by the irresponsible privacy of Slavery. Every Slave-master on his plantation is a Bashaw, with all the prerogatives of a Turk. According to Hobbes, he is a "petty king." This is true; and every plantation is of itself a petty kingdom, with more than the immunities of an abbey. Six thousand skulls of infants are said to have been taken from a single fish-pond near a nunnery, to the dismay of Pope Gregory. Under the law of Slavery, infants, the offspring of masters " who dream of Freedom in a slave's embrace," are not thrown into a fish-pond, but something worse is done. They are sold. But this is only a single glimpse. Slavery, in its recesses, is another Bastile, whose horrors will never be known until it all is razed to the ground; it is the dismal castle of Giant Despair, which, when captured by the Pilgrims, excited their wonder, as they saw "the dead bodies that lay here and there in the castle-yard, and how full of dead men's bones the dungeon was " The recorded horrors of Slavery seem to be infinite, and each day, by the escape of its victims, they are still further attested, while the door of the vast prison-house is left ajar. But, alas! unless the examples of history and the lessons of political wisdom are alike delusive, its unrecorded horrors must assume a form of yet more fearful dimensions, as we try to contemplate them. Baffling all attempts at description, they sink into that chapter of Sir Thomas Browne, entitled, *Of some Relations whose Truth we fear*, and among kindred things whereof, according to this eloquent philosopher, there remains no register but that of hell.

If this picture of the relations of Slave-masters with their slaves could receive any further darkness, it would be by introducing the figures of the congenial agents through which the Barbarism is maintained; *the Slave-overseer, the Slave-breeder, and the Slave-hunter*, each without a peer except in his brother, and the whole constituting the triumvirate of Slavery, in whom its essential brutality, vulgarity, and grossness, are all embodied. There is the Slave-overseer, with his bloody lash, fitly described, in his life of Patrick Henry, by Mr. Wirt, who, born in Virginia, knew the class, as "last and lowest, most abject, degraded, unprincipled," and his hands wield at will the irresponsible power. There is the Slave-breeder, who assumes a higher character, and even enters legislative halls, where, in unconscious insensibility, he shocks civilization by denying, like Mr. Gholson, of Virginia, any alleged distinction between the "female slave" and "the brood mare," by openly asserting the necessary respite from work during the gestation of the female slave as the ground of property in her offspring, and by proclaiming that in this "vigintial" crop of human flesh consists much of the wealth of his State, while another Virginian, not yet hardened to this debasing trade, whose annual sacrifice reaches 25,000 human souls, confesses the indignation and shame with which he beholds his State "converted into *one grand menagerie*, where men are reared for the market, like oxen for the shambles." And lastly there is the Slave-hunter, with the blood-hound as his brutal symbol, who pursues slaves, as the hunter pursues game, and does not hesitate in the public prints to advertise his Barbarism thus:

"BLOOD-HOUNDS.—I have TWO of the FINEST DOGS for CATCHING NE-GROES in the South-west. They can take the trail TWELVE HOURS after the NEGRO HAS PASSED, and catch him with ease. I live four miles south-west of

40

Bolivar, on the road leading from Bolivar to Whitesville.   I am ready at all times to catch runaway negroes.   DAVID TURNER.
"March 2, 1853.— *West-Tennessee Democrat.*"

The blood-hound was known in early Scottish history; it was once vindictively put upon the trail of Robert Bruce, and in barbarous days, by a cruel license of war, it was directed against the marauders of the Scottish border; but more than a century has passed since the last survivor of the race, kept as a curiosity, was fed on meal in Ettrick Forest.*   The blood-hound was employed by Spain, against the natives of this continent, and the eloquence of Chatham never touched a truer chord than when, gathering force from the condemnation of this brutality, he poured his thunder upon the kindred brutality of the scalping-knife, adopted as an instrument of war by a nation professing civilization.   Tardily introduced into our Republic, some time after the Missouri Compromise, when Slavery became a political passion and Slave-masters began to throw aside all disguise, the blood-hound has become the representative of our Barbarism in one of its worst forms, when engaged in the pursuit of a fellow-man who is asserting his inborn title to himself; and this brute is, indeed, typical of the whole brutal leash of Slave-hunters, who, whether at home on Slave-soil, under the name of Slave-catchers, and kidnappers, or at a distance, under politer names, insult Human Nature by the enforcement of this Barbarism.

(3.) From this dreary picture of Slave-masters with their slaves and their triumvirate of vulgar instruments, I pass to another more dreary still, and more completely exposing the influence of Slavery; I mean the *relations of Slave-masters with each other*, also *with Society* and *Government*, or, in other words, the Character of Slave-masters, as displayed in the general relations of life.   And here I need your indulgence.   Not in triumph or in taunt do I approach this branch of the subject.   Yielding only to the irresistible exigency of the discussion and in direct response to the assumptions on this floor, especially by the Senator from Virginia, [Mr. MASON,] I shall proceed.   If I touch Slavery to the quick, and enable Slave-masters to see themselves as others see them, I shall do nothing beyond the strictest line of duty in this debate.

One of the choicest passages of the master Italian poet, Dante,

* Scott's Lay of the Last Minstrel.— *Notes, Canto V.*

41

is where a scene of transcendent virtue is described as sculptured in " visible speech" on the long gallery which led to the Heavenly Gate. The poet felt the inspiration of the scene, and placed it on the way-side, where it could charm and encourage. This was natural. Nobody can look upon virtue and justice, if it be only in images and pictures, without feeling a kindred sentiment. Nobody can be surrounded by vice and wrong, by violence and brutality, if it be only in images and pictures, without coming under their degrading influence. Nobody can live with the one without advantage; nobody can live with the other without loss. Who could pass his life in the secret chamber where are gathered the impure relics of Pompeii, without becoming indifferent to loathsome things? But if these loathsome things are not merely sculptured and painted, if they exist in living reality—if they enact their hideous capers in life, as in the criminal pretensions of Slavery — while the lash plays and the blood spirts—while women are whipped and children are sold—while marriage is polluted and annulled—while the parental tie is rudely torn—while honest gains are filched or robbed—while the soul itself is shut down in all the darkness of ignorance, and while God himself is defied in the pretension that man can have property in his fellow-man; if all these things are present, not merely in images and pictures, but in reality, their influence on character must be incalculable.

It is according to irresistible law that men are fashioned by what is about them, whether climate, scenery, life or institutions. Like produces like, and this ancient proverb is verified always. Look at the miner, delving low down in darkness, and the mountaineer, ranging on airy heights, and you will see a contrast in character, and even in personal form. The difference between a coward and a hero may be traced in the atmosphere which each has breathed; and how much more in the institutions under which each has been reared. If institutions generous and just ripen souls also generous and just, then other institutions must exhibit their influence also. Violence, brutality, injustice, barbarism, must be reproduced in the lives of all who live within their fatal sphere. The meat that is eaten by man enters into and becomes a part of his body; the madder which is eaten by a dog changes his bones to red; and the Slavery on which men live, in all its five-fold foulness, must become a part of themselves, discoloring their very souls, blotting their characters, and breaking forth in moral leprosy. This language is strong; but the evidence is even stronger. Some there may be of happy natures—like honorable Senators—who can thus feed and not be harmed. Mithridates fed on poison, and lived; and it may be that there is a moral Mithridates, who can swallow without bane the poison of Slavery.

Instead of "ennobling" the master, nothing can be clearer than that the slave drags his master down, and this process begins in childhood, and is continued through life. Living much in association with his slave, the master finds nothing to remind him of his own deficiencies, to prompt his ambition or excite his shame. Without these provocations to virtue, and without an elevating example, he naturally shares the Barbarism of the society which he keeps. Thus the very inferiority which the Slave-master attributes to the African race, explains the melancholy condition of the communities in which his degradation is declared by law.

A single false principle or vicious thought may degrade a character otherwise blameless; and this is practically true of the Slave-master. Accustomed to regard men as property, his sensibilities are blunted and his moral sense is obscured. He consents to acts from which Civilization recoils. The early Church sold its property, and even its sacred vessels, for the redemption of captives. This was done on a remarkable occasion by St. Ambrose, and successive canons confirmed the example. But in the Slave States this is all reversed. Slaves there are often sold as the property of the Church, and an instance is related of a slave sold in South-Carolina in order to buy plate for the communion-table. Who can calculate the effect of such an example?

Surrounded by pernicious influences of all kinds, both positive and negative, the first making him do that which he ought not to do, and the second making him leave undone that which he ought to have done—through childhood, youth, and manhood, even unto age—unable while at home to escape these influences, overshadowed constantly by the portentous Barbarism about him, the Slave-master naturally adopts the bludgeon, the revolver and the bowie-knife. Through these he governs his plantation, and secretly armed with these, he enters the world. These are his congenial companions. To wear these is his pride; to use them becomes a passion, almost a necessity. Nothing contributes to violence so much as the wearing of the instruments of violence, thus having them always at hand to obey the lawless instincts of the individual. A barbarous standard is established; a duel is not dishonorable; a contest peculiar to our Slave-masters, known as a "street-fight," is not shameful; and modern imitators of Cain have a mark set upon them, not for reproach and condemnation, but for compliment and approval. I wish to keep within bounds; but unanswerable facts, accmulating in fearful quantities, attest that the social system, so much vaunted by honorable Senators, and which we are now asked to sanction and to extend, takes its character from this spirit, and with professions of Christianity on the lips, becomes Cain-like. And this is aggravated by the prevailing ignorance in the Slave States, where one in twelve of the adult white population is unable to read and write.

> The boldest they who least partake the light,
> As game-cocks in the dark are trained to fight.

Of course there are exceptions, which we all gladly recognize, but it is this spirit which predominates and gives the social law. And here mark an important difference. Elsewhere violence shows itself in *spite* of law, whether social or statute; in the Slave States it is *because* of law both social and statute. Elsewhere it is pursued and condemned; in the Slave States it is adopted and honored. Elsewhere it is hunted as a crime; in the Slave States it takes its place among the honorable graces of society.

Let not these harsh statements stand on my authority. Listen to the testimony of two Governors of Slave States in their messages to the Legislatures:

"We long to see the day," said the Governor of Kentucky in 1837, "when the law will assert its majesty, and stop the wanton destruction of life which almost *daily* occurs within the jurisdiction of the Commonwealth. *Men slaughter each other with almost perfect impunity.* A species of common law has grown up in Kentucky, which, were it written down, would, in all civilized countries, cause it to be rechristened, in derision, *the land of blood.*"

Such was the official confession of a Slave-master Governor of Kentucky. And here is the official confession made the same year by the Slave-master Governor of Alabama:

"We hear of homicides in different parts of the State continually, and yet have

44

few convictions, and still fewer executions! Why do we hear of *stabbings and shootings* almost *daily* in some part or other of our State?"

A land of blood! Stabbings and shootings almost daily! Such is the official language. It was natural that contemporary newspapers should repeat what thus found utterance in high places. Here is a confession by a newspaper in Mississippi:

"The moral atmosphere in our State appears to be in a *deleterious and sanguinary condition.* Almost every exchange paper which reaches us contains *some inhuman and revolting case of murder or death by violence.*"—*Grand Gulf Advertiser*, 27th *June*, 1837.

Here is another confession by a newspaper in New-Orleans:

"In view of the crimes which are daily committed, we are led to inquire whether it is owing to the inefficiency of our laws, or to the manner in which these laws are administered, *that this frightful deluge of human blood flows through our streets and our places of public resort.*"—*New-Orleans Bee*, 23d *May*, 1838.

And here is testimony of a different character:

"No one who has not been *an integral part of a slaveholding community* can have any idea of its abominations. It is a whited sepulchre, full of dead men's bones and all uncleanness."

These are the words of a Southern lady, the daughter of the accomplished Judge Grimké of South-Carolina.

A catalogue of affrays between politicians, commonly known as "street-fights"—I use the phrase which comes from the land of Slavery—would show that these authorities were not mistaken. That famous Dutch picture, admired particularly by a successful engraving, and called the *Knife-fight*, presents a scene less revolting than one of these. Two or more men, armed to the teeth, meet in the streets, at a court house or a tavern, shoot at each other with revolvers, then gash each other with knives, close, and roll upon the ground, covered with dirt and blood, struggling and stabbing till death, prostration, or surrender puts an end to the conflict. Each instance tells a shameful story, and cries out against the social system which can tolerate such Barbarism. A catalogue of duels in our country would testify again to the reckless disregard of life where Slavery exists, and would exhibit Violence flaunting in the garb of Honor, and prating of a barbarous code disowned equally by reason and religion. But you have already supped too full of horrors, and I hasten on.

Pardon me if I stop for one moment to exhibit and denounce the Duel. I do it only because it belongs to the brood of Slavery. An enlightened Civilization has long ago rejected this relic of Barbarism, and never has one part of the argument against it been put more sententiously than by Franklin: "A duel decides nothing," said this patriot philosopher, "and the person appealing to it makes himself judge in his own cause, condemns the offender without a jury, and undertakes himself to be the executioner." To these emphatic words I would add two brief propositions, which, if practically adopted, make the Duel impossible. First, that the acknowledgment of wrong with apology or explanation can never be otherwise than honorable; and, secondly, that, in the absence of all such acknowledgment, no wrong can ever be repaired by a gladiatorial contest, where brute force, or skill, or chance, must decide the day. Iron and adamant are not stronger than these arguments; nor can any one attempt an answer without exposing his feebleness. And yet Slave-masters, disregarding its irrational character, insensible to its folly, heedless of its impiety, and unconscious of its Barbarism, openly adopt the Duel as a regulator of manners and conduct. Two voices from South-Carolina have been raised against it, and I mention them with gladness as testimony even in that land of Slavery. The first was Charles Cotesworth Pinckney, who, in the early days of the Republic, openly declared his "abhorrence of the practice," and invoked the clergy of his State "as a particular favor, at some convenient early day, to preach a sermon on the sin and folly of dueling." The other was Mr. Rhett, who, on this floor, openly declared as his reason for declining the duel, "that he feared God more than man." Generous words, for which many errors can be pardoned. But these voices condemn the social system of which the Duel is a natural product.

Looking now at the broad surface of society where Slavery exists, we shall find its spirit actively manifest in the suppression of all freedom of speech or of the press, especially with regard to this wrong. Nobody in the Slave States can speak or print against Slavery, except at the peril of life or liberty. St. Paul could call upon the people of Athens to give up the worship of unknown gods; he could live in his own hired house at Rome, and preach Christianity in this Heathen metropolis; but no man can be heard against Slavery in Charleston or Mobile. We condemn the Inquisition, which subjects all within its influence to censorship and secret-judgment; but this tyranny is repeated in American Slave-masters. Truths as simple as the great discovery of Galileo are openly denied, and all who declare them are driven to recant. We condemn the Index Expurgatorius of the Roman Church; but American Slave-masters have an Index on which are inscribed all the generous books of the age. There is one book, the marvel of recent literature, Uncle Tom's Cabin, which has been thus treated both by the Church and by the Slave-masters, so that it is honored by the same suppression at the Vatican and at Charleston.

Not to dwell on these instances, there is one which has a most instructive ridiculousness. A religious discourse of the late Dr. Channing on West-India Emancipation—the last effort of his beautiful career—was offered for sale by a book agent at Charleston. A prosecution by the South-Carolina Association ensued, and the agent was held to bail in the sum of one thousand dollars. Shortly afterward, the same agent received for sale a work by Dickens, freshly published, "American Notes;" but, determined not to expose himself again to the tyrannical Inquisition, he gave notice through the newspapers that the book " would be submitted to highly intelligent members of the South-Carolina Association for *inspection*, and *if* the sale is approved by them, it will be for sale—if not, not."

Listen also to another recent instance, as recounted in the *Montgomery Mail*, a newspaper of Alabama:

"Last Saturday we devoted to the flames a large number of copies of Spurgeon's Sermons, and the pile was graced at the top with a copy of ' Graves's Great Iron Wheel,' which a Baptist friend presented for the purpose. We trust that the works of the greasy cockney vociferator may receive the same treatment throughout the South. And if the Pharisaical author should ever show himself in these parts, we trust that a stout cord may speedily find its way around his eloquent throat. He has proved himself a dirty, low-bred slanderer, and ought to be treated accordingly."

And very recently we have read in the journals, that the trustees of a College in Alabama have resolved that Dr. Wayland's admirable work on Moral Science " contains abolition doctrine of the deepest dye;" and they proceeded to denounce "the said book, and forbid its further use in the Institute."

The speeches of Wilberforce in the British Parliament, and especially those magnificent efforts of Brougham, where he exposed "the wild and guilty fantasy that man can hold property in man," were insanely denounced by the British planters in the West-Indies; but our Slave-masters go further. Speeches delivered in the Senate have been stopped at the Post-Office; booksellers who had received them have been mobbed, and on at least one occasion the speeches have been solemnly proceeded against by a Grand Jury.

All this is natural, for tyranny is condemned to be consequent with itself. Proclaim Slavery to be a permanent institution, instead of a temporary Barbarism, soon to pass away, and then, by the unhesitating logic of self-preservation, all things must yield to its support. The safety of Slavery becomes the supreme law. And since Slavery is endangered by liberty in any form, therefore all liberty must be restrained. Such is the philosophy of this seeming paradox in a Republic. And our Slave-masters show themselves apt in this work. Violence and brutality are their ready instruments, quickened always by the wakefulness of suspicion, and perhaps often by the restlessness of uneasy conscience. Everywhere in the Slave States the Lion's Mouth of Venice, where citizens were anonymously denounced, is open; nor are the gloomy prisons and the Bridge of Sighs wanting.

This spirit has recently shown itself with such intensity and activity as to constitute what has been properly termed a reign of terror. Northern men, unless they happen to be delegates to a Democratic Convention, are exposed in their travels, whether of business or health, to the operation of this system. They are watched and dogged, as if in a land of Despotism; they are treated with the meanness of a disgusting tyranny, and live in peril always of personal indignity, and often of life and limb. Complaint has sometimes been made of the wrongs to American citizens in Mexico; but during the last year, more outrages on American citizens have been perpetrated in the Slave States than in Mexico. Here, again, I have no time for details, which have been already presented in other quarters. But the instances are from all conditions of life. In Missouri, a Methodist clergyman, suspected of being an Abolitionist, was taken to prison, amidst threats of tar and feathers. In Arkansas, a schoolmaster was driven from the State. In Kentucky, a plain citizen from Indiana, on a visit to his friends, was threatened with death by the rope. In Alabama, a simple person from Connecticut, peddling books, was thrust into prison, amidst cries of "Shoot him! hang him!" In Virginia, a Shaker, from

New-York, peddling garden-seeds, was forcibly expelled from the State. In Georgia, a merchant's clerk, Irishman by birth, who simply asked the settlement of a just debt, was cast into prison, robbed of his pocket-book, containing nearly one hundred dollars, and barely escaped with his life. In South-Carolina, a stone-cutter, Irishman by birth, was stripped naked, and then, amidst cries of "Brand him!" "Burn him!" "Spike him to death!" scourged so that blood came at every stroke, while tar was poured upon his lacerated flesh. These atrocities, calculated, according to the words of a poet of subtle beauty, to "make a holiday in hell," were all ordained, by Vigilance Committees, or by that busiest magistrate, Judge Lynch, inspired by the demon of Slavery.

> "He let them loose, and cried, Halloo!
> How shall we yield him honor due?"

In perfect shamelessness, and as if to blazon this fiendish spirit, we have had, this winter, in a leading newspaper of Virginia, an article, proposing to give twenty-five dollars each for the heads of citizens, mostly members of Congress, known to be against Slavery, and $50,000 for the head of William H. Seward. And in still another paper of Virginia, we find a proposition to raise $10,000 to be given for the kidnapping and delivery of a venerable citizen, Joshua R. Giddings, at Richmond, "or $5000 for the production of his head." These are fresh instances, but they are not alone. At a meeting of Slave-masters in Georgia, in 1835, the Governor was recommended to issue a proclamation, offering $5000 as a reward for the apprehension of *either* of ten persons named in the resolution, citizens of New-York and Massachusetts, and one a subject of Great Britain—not one of whom it was pretended had ever set foot on the soil of Georgia. The Milledgeville *Federal Union*, a newspaper of Georgia, in 1836, contained an offer of $10,000 for kidnapping a clergyman residing in the city of New-York. A Committee of Vigilance of Louisiana, in 1835, offered, in the *Louisiana Journal*, $50,000 to any person who would deliver into their hands Arthur Tappan, a merchant of New-York; and during the same year a public meeting in Alabama, with a person entitled "Honorable" in the chair, offered a similar reward of $50,000 for the apprehension of the same Arthur Tappan, and of La Roy Sunderland, a clergyman of the Methodist Church at New-York.

These manifestations are not without prototype in the history of the Anti-Slavery cause in other countries. From the beginning, Slave-masters have encountered argument by brutality and violence. If we go back to the earliest of Abolitionists, the wonderful Portuguese preacher, Vieyra, we shall find that his matchless eloquence and unquestioned piety did not save him from indignity. After a sermon exposing Slavery in Brazil, he was seized and imprisoned, while one of the principal Slave-masters asked him, in mockery, where were all his learning and all his genius now, if they could not deliver him in this extremity? He was of the Catholic Church. But the spirit of Slavery is the same in all churches. A renowned Quaker minister of the last century, Thomas Chalkley, while on a visit at Barbadoes, having simply recommended charity to the slaves, without presuming to breathe a word against Slavery itself, was first met by disturbance in the meeting, and afterward, on the highway, and in open day, was fired at by one of the exasperated planters, with "a fowling-piece loaded with small shot, ten of which made marks, and several drew blood." Even in England, while the slave-trade was under discussion, the same spirit appeared. Wilberforce, who represented the cause of Abolition in Parliament, was threatened with personal violence; Clarkson, who represented the same cause before the people, was assaulted by the infuriate Slave-traders, and narrowly escaped being hustled into the dock; and Roscoe, the accomplished historian, on his return to Liverpool from his seat in Parliament, where he had signalized himself as an opponent of the Slave-trade, was met at the entrance of the town by a savage mob, composed of persons interested in this traffic, armed with *knives and bludgeons*, the distinctive arguments and companions of Pro-Slavery partisans.

And even in the Free States the partisans of Slavery have, from the beginning, acted under the inspiration of violence. The demon of Slavery has entered into them, and under its influence they have behaved like Slave-masters. Public meetings for the discussion of Slavery have been interrupted; public halls, dedicated to its discussion, have been destroyed or burned to the ground. In all our populous cities the great rights of speech and of the press have been assailed precisely as in the

Slave States. In Boston, Garrison, pleading for the Slave, was dragged through the streets with a halter about his neck; and in Illinois Lovejoy, also pleading for the Slave, was ferociously murdered. The former yet lives to speak for himself, while the latter lives in his eloquent brother, the Representative from Illinois in the other House. Thus does Slavery show its natural influence even at a distance.

Nor in the Slave States is this spirit confined to the outbreaks of mere lawlessness. Too strong for restraint, it finds no limitations except in its own barbarous will. The Government becomes its tool, and in *official acts* does its bidding. Here again the instances are numerous. I might dwell on the degradation of the Post-Office, when its official head consented that, for the sake of Slavery, the mails themselves should be rifled. I might dwell also on the cruel persecution of Free Persons of color who in the Slave States generally, and even here in the District of Columbia, are not allowed to testify where a white man is in question, and who now in several States are menaced by legislative act with the alternative of expulsion from their homes or of reduction to Slavery. But I pass at once to two illustrative transactions, which, as a son of Massachusetts, I can not forget.

1. The first relates to a citizen of purest life and perfect integrity, whose name is destined to fill a conspicuous place in the history of Freedom, William Lloyd Garrison. Born in Massachusetts, bred to the same profession with Benjamin Franklin, and like his great predecessor becoming an editor, he saw with instinctive clearness the wrong of Slavery, and at a period when the ardors of the Missouri Question had given way to indifference throughout the North, he stepped forward to denounce it. The jail at Baltimore, where he then resided, was his earliest reward. Afterward, January 1st, 1831, he published the first number of the *Liberator*, inscribing for his motto an utterance of Christian philanthropy, "My country is the world, my countrymen are all mankind," and declaring in the face of surrounding apathy: "I am in earnest. I will not equivocate, I will not retreat a single inch, and I will be heard." In this sublime spirit he commenced his labors for the Slave, proposing no intervention by Congress in the States, and on well-considered principle avoiding all appeals to the bondmen themselves. Such was his simple and thoroughly constitutional position,

51

when, before the expiration of the first year, the Legislature of Georgia, by solemn act, a copy of which I have now before me, "approved" by Wilson Lumpkin, Governor, appropriated $5000 "to be paid to any person who shall arrest, bring to trial, and prosecute to conviction under the laws of this State, the editor or publisher of a certain paper called the *Liberator*, published at the town of Boston and State of Massachusetts." This infamous legislative act touching a person absolutely beyond the jurisdiction of Georgia, and in no way amenable to its laws, constituted a plain bribe to the gangs of kidnappers engendered by Slavery. With this barefaced defiance of justice and decency Slave-masters inaugurated the system of violence by which they have sought to crush every voice that has been raised against Slavery.

2. Here is another illustration of a different character. Free persons of color, citizens of Massachusetts, and, according to the institutions of this Commonwealth, entitled to equal privileges with other citizens, being in service as mariners, and touching at the port of Charleston, in South-Carolina, have been seized, and with no allegation against them, except of entering this port in the discharge of their rightful business, have been cast into prison, and there detained during the delay of the vessel. This is by virtue of a statute of South-Carolina, passed in 1823, which further declares, that in the failure of the captain to pay the expenses, these freemen "shall be seized and taken as absolute slaves," one moiety of the proceeds of their sale to belong to the Sheriff. Against all remonstrance — against the official opinion of Mr. Wirt, as Attorney-General of the United States, declaring it unconstitutional — against the solemn judgment of Mr. Justice Johnson, of the Supreme Court of the United States, himself a Slave-master and citizen of South-Carolina, also pronouncing it unconstitutional — this statute, which is an obvious injury to Northern ship-owners, as it is an outrage to the mariners whom it seizes, has been upheld to this day by South-Carolina.

But this is not all. Massachusetts, in order to obtain for her citizens that protection which was denied, and especially to save them from the dread penalty of being sold into Slavery, appointed a citizen of South-Carolina to act as her agent for this purpose, and to bring suits in the Circuit Court of the United States in order to try the constitutionality of this pretension.

Owing to the sensibility of the people in that State, this agent declined to render this simple service. Massachusetts next selected one of her own sons, a venerable citizen, who had already served with honor in the other House of Congress, and who was of admitted eminence as a lawyer, the Hon. Samuel Hoar, of Concord, to visit Charleston, and to do what the agent first appointed had shrunk from doing. This excellent gentleman, beloved by all who knew him, gentle in manners as he was firm in character, and with a countenance that was in itself a letter of recommendation, arrived at Charleston, accompanied only by his daughter. Straightway all South-Carolina was convulsed. According to a story in Boswell's Johnson, all the inhabitants at St. Kilda, a remote island of the Hebrides, on the approach of a stranger, "catch cold;" but in South-Carolina it is a fever that they "catch." The Governor at the time, who was none other than one of her present Senators, [Mr. HAMMOND,] made his arrival the subject of a special message to the Legislature, which I now have before me; the Legislature all "caught" the fever, and swiftly adopted resolutions calling upon "his Excellency the Governor to expel from its territory the said agent, after due notice to depart," and promising "to sustain the Executive authority in any measures it may adopt for the purposes aforesaid."

Meanwhile the fever raged in Charleston. The agent of Massachusetts was first accosted in the streets by a person unknown to him, who, flourishing a bludgeon in his hand — the bludgeon always shows itself where Slavery is in question — cried out: "You had better be traveling, and the sooner the better for you, I can tell you; if you stay here until to-morrow morning, you will feel something you will not like, I'm thinking." Next came threats of an attack during the following night on the hotel in which he was lodged; then a request from the landlord that he should quit, in order to preserve the hotel itself from the impending danger of an infuriated mob; then a committee of Slave-masters, who politely proposed to conduct him to the boat. Thus arrested in his simple errand of goodwill, this venerable public servant, whose appearance alone — like that of the "grave and pious man" mentioned by Virgil — would have softened any mob not inspired by Slavery, yielded to the ejectment proposed — precisely as the prisoner yields to the officers of the law — and left Charleston, while a person in the crowd was heard to offer himself as "the leader of a tar-and-feather gang, to be called into the service of the city on the occasion." Nor is this all. The Legislature a second time "caught" the fever, and, yielding to its influence, passed another statute, forbidding, under severe penalties, any person within the State from accepting a commission to befriend these colored mariners; and under penalties severer still, extending even to imprisonment for life, prohibiting any person "on his own behalf, or by virtue of any authority from any State," to come within South-Carolina for this purpose; and then, to complete its work, the Legislature took away the writ of *habeas corpus* from all such mariners.

Such is a simple narrative, founded on authentic documents. I do not adduce it now for criticism, but simply to enroll it in all its stages—beginning with the earliest pretension of South-Carolina, continuing in violence, and ending in yet other pretensions—among the special instances where the Barbarism of Slavery stands confessed even in official conduct. And yet this transaction, which may well give to South-Carolina the character of a shore "where shipwrecked mariners dread to land," has been openly vindicated in all its details from beginning to end by both the Senators from that State, while one of them, [Mr. HAMMOND,] in the same breath, has borne his testimony from personal knowledge to the character of the public agent thus maltreated, saying: "He was a pleasant, kind old gentleman, and I had a sort of friendship for him during the short time I sat near him in Congress.

Thus, sir, whether we look at individuals, or at the community where Slavery exists, at lawless outbreaks or at official conduct, Slave-masters are always the same. Enough, you will say, has been said. Yes; enough to expose Slavery, but not enough for Truth. The most instructive and most grievous part still remains. It is the exhibition of Slave-masters in Congressional history. Of course, the representative reflects the character as well as the political opinions of the constituents, whose will it is his boast to obey. It follows that the passions and habits of Slave-masters are naturally represented in Congress—chastened to a certain extent, perhaps, by the requirements of Parliamentary Law, but breaking out in fearful examples. And here, again, facts shall speak, as nothing else can.

In proceeding with this duty, to which, as you will perceive, I am impelled by the positive requirements of this debate, I crave the indulgence of the Senate, while, avoiding all allusions to private life or private character, and touching simply what is of record, and already "enrolled in the Capitol," I present a few only of many instances, which, especially during these latter days, since Slavery has become paramount, have taken their place in our national history.

Here is an instance. On the 15th February, 1837, R. M. Whitney was arraigned before the House of Representatives, for contempt, in refusing to attend, when required, before a Committee of investigation into the administration of the Executive office. His excuse was, that he could not attend without exposing himself thereby to outrage and violence in the committee-room; and on examination at the bar of the House, Mr. Fairfield, a member of the Committee, afterward a member of this body, and Governor of Maine, testified to the actual facts. It appeared that Mr. Peyton, a Slave-master from Tennessee, and a member of the Committee, regarding a certain answer in writing by Mr. Whitney to an interrogatory propounded by him as offensive, broke out in these words: "Mr. Chairman, I wish you to inform this witness, that he is not to insult me in his answers; if he does, God damn him! I will take his life on the spot!" The witness, rising, claimed the protection of the Committee; on which Mr. Peyton exclaimed: "God damn you, you shan't speak; you shan't say one word while you are in this room; if you do, I will put you to death." Mr. Wise, another Slave-master from Virginia, Chairman of the Committee, and latterly Governor of Virginia, then intervened, saying: "Yes, this damned insolence is insufferable." Soon after, Mr. Peyton, observing that the witness was looking at him, cried out: "Damn him, his eyes are on me; God damn him, he is looking at me; he shan't do it; damn him, he shan't look at me."

These things, and much more, disclosed by Mr. Fairfield, in reply to interrogatories in the House, were confirmed by other witnesses; and Mr. Wise himself, in a speech, made the admission, that he was armed with deadly weapons, saying: "I watched the motion of that right arm, [of the witness,] the elbow of which could be seen by me, and had it moved one inch, he had died on the spot. That was my determination."

All this will be found in the thirteenth volume of the *Congressional Debates*, with the evidence in detail, and the discussion thereupon.

Here is another instance of similar character, which did not occur in a committee-room, but during debate in the Senate Chamber. While the Compromise measures were under discussion, in 1850, on the 17th of April, 1850, Mr. Foote, a Slave-master from Mississippi, in the course of his remarks, commenced a personal allusion to Mr. Benton. This was aggravated by the circumstance that only a few days previously he had made this distinguished gentleman the mark for most bitter and vindictive personalities. Mr. Benton rose at once from his seat, and, with an angry countenance, but without weapons of any kind in his hand, or, as it appeared afterward before the Committee, on his person, advanced in the direction of Mr. Foote, when the latter, gliding backward, drew from his pocket a five-chambered revolver, full loaded, which he cocked. Meanwhile Mr. Benton, at the suggestion of friends, was already returning to his seat, when he perceived the pistol. Excited greatly by this deadly menace, he exclaimed: "I am not armed. I have no pistols. I disdain to carry arms. Stand out of the way, and let the assassin fire." Mr. Foote remained standing in the position he had taken, with his pistol in his hand, cocked. "Soon after," says the report of the Committee appointed to investigate this occurrence, "both Senators resumed their seats, and order was restored."

All this will be found at length in the 21st volume of the *Congressional Globe*.

Another instance, which belongs to the same class, is given by the Hon. William Jay, a writer of singular accuracy, and of the truest principle, who has done much to illustrate the history of our country. It is this: Mr. Dawson, a Slave-master from Louisiana, and a member of the House of Representatives, went up to another member on the floor of the House, and addressed to him these words: "If you attempt to speak, or rise from your seat, sir, by G—d, I'll cut your throat."

The duel, which at home in the Slave States is "twin" with

the "street-fight," is also "twin" with these instances. It is constantly adopted or attempted by Slave-masters in Congress. But I shall not enter upon this catalogue. I content myself with showing the openness with which in debate it has been menaced, and without any call to order.

Mr. Foote, the same Slave-master already mentioned, in debate in the Senate, 26th of March, 1850, thus sought to provoke Mr. Benton. I take his words from the *Congressional Globe*, vol. 21, p. 603:

> "There are instances in the history of the Senator which might well relieve a man of honor from the obligation to recognize him as a fitting antagonist; yet it is notwithstanding true, that, if the Senator from Missouri will deign to acknowledge himself *responsible to the laws of honor*, he shall have a very early opportunity of proving his prowess in contest with one over whom I hold perfect control; or, if he feels in the least degree aggrieved at any thing which has fallen from me, he shall, on demanding it, *have full redress accorded to him*, according to the said laws of honor. I do not denounce him as a coward; such language is unfitted for this audience; but if he wishes to patch up his reputation for courage, now greatly on the wane, he will certainly *have an opportunity of doing so whenever he makes his desire known in the premises.* At present he is shielded by his age, *his open disavowal of the obligatory laws of honor,* and his senatorial privileges."

With such bitter taunts and reïterated provocations to the duel was Mr. Benton pursued; but there was no call to order, nor any action of the Senate on this outrage.

Here is another instance. In debate in the Senate on the 27th February, 1852, Mr. Clemens, a Slave-master of Alabama, thus directly attacked Mr. Rhett, for undertaking to settle their differences by argument in the Senate, rather than by the Duel. "No man," said he, "with the feeling of a man in his bosom, would have sought redress here. He would have looked for it *elsewhere.* He now comes here not to ask redress in the only way he should have sought it."

There was no call to order.

Here is still another. In the debate of the bill for the improvement of Rivers and Harbors, 29th July, 1854, (*Congressional Globe*, vol. 29, appendix, page 1163,) the Senator from Louisiana, [Mr. BENJAMIN,] who is still a member of this body, ardent for Slavery, while professing to avoid personal altercation in the Senate, especially "with a gentleman who professes the principles of non-resistance, as he understood the Senator from New-York does," proceeded most earnestly to repel an imagined imputation on him by Mr. Seward, and wound up by saying: "If it came from another quarter, *it would not be upon this floor that I should answer it.*"

And then, during the present session, the Senator from Mississippi, [Mr. DAVIS,] who speaks so often for Slavery, in a colloquy on this floor with the Senator from Vermont, [Mr. COLLAMER,] has maintained the Duel as a mode of settling personal differences, and vindicating what is called personal honor; as if personal honor did not depend absolutely upon what a man does, and not what is done to him. "A gentleman," says the Senator, "has the right to give an insult, *if he feels himself bound to answer for it;*" and in reply to the Senator from Vermont, he declared, that in case of insult, taking another out and shooting him might be "satisfaction."

I do not dwell on this instance, nor on any of these instances, except to make a single comment. These declarations have all been made in open Senate, without any check from the Chair. Of course, they are clear violations of the first principles of Parliamentary Law, and tend directly to provoke a violation of the law of the land. All duels are prohibited by solemn act of Congress. (See Statutes at Large, vol. 5, page 318, February 20, 1839.) In case of death, the surviving parties are declared guilty of felony, to be punished by hard labor in the penitentiary; and, even where nothing has occurred beyond the challenge, all the parties to it, whether givers or receivers, are declared guilty of high crime and misdemeanor, also to be punished by hard labor in the penitentiary. Of course, every menace of a duel in Congress sets this law at defiance. And yet the Senators, who thus openly disregard a law sanctioned by the Constitution and commended by morality, presume to complain on this floor because other Senators disregard the Fugitive Slave Bill, a statute which, according to the profound convictions of large numbers, is as unconstitutional as it is offensive to the moral sense. Let Senators who are so clamorous for "the enforcement of laws," begin by enforcing the statute which declares the Duel to be a felony. At least, let the statute cease to be a dead letter in this Chamber. But this is too much to expect while Slavery prevails here, for the Duel is a part of that System of Violence which has its origin in Slavery.

But it is when aroused by the Slave question in Congress that Slave-masters have most truly shown themselves; and here again I shall speak only of what has already passed into history. Even in that earliest debate, in the First Congress after the Constitution, on the memorial of Dr. Franklin, simply calling upon Congress "to step to the verge of its powers to discourage every species of traffic in our fellow-men," the Slave-masters became angry, indulged in sneers at "the men in the gallery" being Quakers and Abolitionists, and, according to the faithful historian, Hildreth, poured out "torrents of abuse," while one of them began the charge so often since directed against all Anti-Slavery men, by declaring his astonishment that Dr. Franklin had "given countenance to an application which called upon Congress, in explicit terms, to break a solemn compact to which he had himself been a party," when it was obvious that Dr. Franklin had done no such thing. This great man was soon summoned away by death, but not until he had fastened upon this debate an undying condemnation, by portraying, with his matchless pen, a scene in the Divan at Algiers, where a corsair Slave-dealer, insisting upon the enslavement of White Christians, is made to repeat the Congressional speech of an American Slave-master.

But these displays of Violence have naturally increased with the intensity of the discussion. Impelled to be severe, but with little appreciation of the finer forms of debate, they could not be severe except by violating the rules of debate; not knowing that there is a serener power than any found in personalities, and that all severity which transcends the rules of debate becomes disgusting as the talk of Yahoos, and harms him only who degrades himself to be its mouth-piece. Of course, on such occasions, the cause of Slavery, amidst all seeming triumphs, has lost, and Truth has gained.

It was against John Quincy Adams that this violence was first directed in full force. To a character spotless as snow, and to universal attainments as a scholar, this illustrious citizen added experience in all the eminent posts of the Republic, which he had filled with an ability and integrity, now admitted even by his enemies, and which impartial history can not forget. Having been President of the United States, he entered the House of Representatives at the period when the Slave Question in its revival first began to occupy the public attention. In all the completeness of his nature, he became the representative of

Human Freedom. The first struggle occurred on the right of petition, which Slave-masters with characteristic tyranny sought to suppress. This was resisted by the venerable patriot, and what he did was always done with his whole heart. Then was poured upon him abuse *as from a cart.* Slave-masters, "foaming out their shame," became conspicuous, not less for an avowal of sentiments at which Civilization blushed, than for an effrontery of manner where the accidental legislator was lost in the natural overseer, and the lash of the plantation resounded in the voice.

In an address to his constituents, 17th September, 1842, Mr. Adams thus frankly describes the treatment he had experienced:

" I never can take part in any debate upon an important subject, be it only upon a mere abstraction, but a pack opens upon me of personal invective in return. Language has no word of reproach and railing that is not hurled at me."

And in the same speech he gives a glimpse of Slave-masters:

" Where the South can not effect her object by brow-beating, she wheedles."

On another occasion he said, with his accustomed power:

" Insult, bullying, and threat, characterize the Slaveholders in Congress; talk, timidity, and submission the Representatives from the Free States."

Nor were the Slave-masters contented with the violence of words. True to the instincts of Slavery, they threatened personal indignity of every kind, and even assassination. And here South-Carolina naturally took the lead.

The *Charleston Mercury,* which always speaks the true voice of Slavery, said in 1837:

" Public opinion in the South would now, we are sure, justify an immediate resort to force by the Southern delegation, *even on the floor of Congress,* were they forthwith to seize and drag from the Hall any man who dared to insult them, as that eccentric old showman, John Quincy Adams, has dared to do."

And at a public dinner at Walterborough, in South Carolina, on the 4th of July, 1842, the following toast, afterwards preserved by Mr. Adams in one of his speeches, was drunk with unbounded applause:

" May we never want a Democrat to trip up the heels of a Federalist, or a hangman to prepare a halter for John Quincy Adams! [Nine cheers.]"

A Slave-master from South-Carolina, Mr. Waddy Thompson, in debate in the House of Representatives, threatened the venerable patriot with the "penitentiary;" and another Slave master, Mr. Marshall of Kentucky, insisted that he should be "*silenced.*" Ominous word! full of suggestion to the bludgeon-bearers of Slavery. But the great representative of Freedom stood firm. Meanwhile Slavery assumed more and more the port of the giant Maul in the Pilgrim's Progress, who continued with his club breaking the skulls of pilgrims, until he was slain by Mr. Great Heart, making way for the other Pilgrims, Mr. Valiant for Truth, Mr. Standfast, and Mr. Honest.

Next to John Quincy Adams, no person in Congress has been more conspicuous for long-continued and patriotic services against Slavery, than Joshua R. Giddings, of Ohio; nor have any such services received in higher degree that homage which is found in the personal and most vindictive assaults of Slave-masters. For nearly twenty years he sat in the House of Representatives, bearing his testimony always loftily, and never shrinking, though exposed to the grossest brutality. In a recent public address at New-York, he has himself recounted some of these instances.

On the presentation by him of resolutions affirming that Slavery was a local institution, and could not exist outside of the Slave States, and applying this principle to the case of the Creole, the House "caught" the South-Carolina fever. A proposition censuring him was introduced by Slave-masters and pressed to a vote, under the operation of the previous question, without giving him a moment for explanation or reply. This glaring outrage upon freedom of debate was redressed at once by the constituency of Mr. Giddings, who returned him again to his seat. From that time the rage of the Slave-masters against him was constant. Here is his own brief account:

"I will not speak of the time when Dawson, of Louisiana, drew a bowie-knife for my assassination. I was afterward speaking with regard to a certain transaction in which negroes were concerned in Georgia, when Mr. Black, of Georgia, raising his bludgeon, and standing in front of my seat, said to me: 'If you repeat that language again, I will knock you down.' It was a solemn moment for me. I had never been knocked down, and having some curiosity upon that subject, I repeated the language. Then Mr. Dawson, of Louisiana, the same who had drawn the bowie-knife, placed his hand in his pocket and said, with an oath which I will not repeat, that he would shoot me, at the same time cocking the pistol, so that all around me could hear it click."

Listening to these horrors, ancient stories of Barbarism seem all outdone; and the "viper broth," which was a favorite decoction in a barbarous age, seems to have become the daily drink of American Slave-masters. The blaspheming madness of the witches in Macbeth, dancing round the cauldron, and dropping into it "sweltered venom sleeping got," and every other "charm of powerful trouble," was all renewed. But Mr. Giddings, strong in the consciousness of right, knew the dignity of his position. He knew that it is honorable always to serve the cause of Liberty, and that it is a privilege to suffer for this cause. Reproach, contumely, violence even unto death, are rewards, not punishments; and clearly the indignities which you offer can excite no shame except for their authors.

Besides these eminent instances, others may be mentioned, showing the personalities to which Senators and Representatives have been exposed, when undertaking to speak for Freedom. And truth compels me to add, that there is too much evidence that these have been aggravated by the circumstance that, where persons notoriously rejected an appeal to the Duel, such insults could be offered with impunity.

Here is an instance. In 1848, Mr. HALE, the Senator from New-Hampshire, who still continues an honor to this body, introduced into the Senate a bill for the protection of property in the District of Columbia, especially against mob-violence. In the course of the debate that ensued, Mr. Foote, a Slave-master from Mississippi, thus menaced him:

> "I invite the Senator to the State of Mississippi, and will tell him beforehand, in all honesty, that he could not go ten miles into the interior before he would grace one of the tallest trees of the forest with a rope around his neck, with the approbation of every virtuous and patriotic citizen, and that, if necessary, *I should myself assist in the operation.*"

That this bloody threat may not seem to stand alone, I add two others.

Mr. HAMMOND, of South-Carolina, now a Senator, is reported as saying in the House of Representatives:

> "I warn the abolitionists, ignorant, infatuated barbarians as they are, that if chance shall throw any of them into our hands, they may expect *a felon's death!*"

And in 1841, Mr. PAYNE, a Slave-master from Alabama, in the course of debate in the House of Representatives, alluding to the Abolitionists, among whom he insisted the Postmaster-General ought to be included, declared that

> "He would put the brand of Cain upon them—yes, the mark of hell—and if they came to the South he would *hang them like dogs.*"

62

And these words were applied to men who simply expressed the recorded sentiments of Washington, Jefferson and Franklin.

Even during the present session of Congress, I find in the *Congressional Globe* the following interruptions of Mr. LOVEJOY, when speaking on Slavery. I do not characterize them, but simply cite them :

By Mr. BARKSDALE, of Mississippi:

"Order that black-hearted scoundrel and nigger-stealing thief to take his seat."

By Mr. BOYCE, of South-Carolina, addressing Mr. LOVEJOY:

"Then behave yourself."

By Mr. GARTRELL, of Georgia, (in his seat:)

"The man is crazy."

By Mr. BARKSDALE, of Mississippi, again :

"No, sir, you stand there to-day an infamous, perjured villain."

By Mr. ASHMORE, of South-Carolina :

"Yes; he is a perjured villain, and he perjures himself every hour he occupies a seat on this floor."

By Mr. SINGLETON, of Mississippi :

"And a negro-thief into the bargain."

By Mr. BARKSDALE, of Mississippi, again :

"I hope my colleague will hold no parley with that perjured negro-thief."

By Mr. SINGLETON of Mississippi, again :

"No, sir; any gentleman shall have time, but not such a mean, despicable wretch as that!"

By Mr. MARTIN, of Virginia :

"And if you come among us, we will do with you as we did with John Brown— hang you as high as Haman. I say that as a Virginian."

But enough — enough ; and I now turn from this branch of the argument with a single remark. While exhibiting the Character of Slave-masters, these numerous instances—and they might be multiplied indefinitely — attest the weakness of their cause. It requires no special talent to estimate the insignificance of an argument that can be supported only by violence. The scholar will not forget the story told by Lucian of the colloquy between Jupiter and a simple countryman. They talked with ease and freedom until they differed, when the angry god at once menaced his honest opponent with a thunder-bolt. "Ah! ah!" said the clown, with perfect composure, "now, Jupiter, I know you are wrong. You are always wrong when you ap-

63

peal to your thunder." And permit me to say, that every appeal, whether to the Duel, the bludgeon, or the revolver—every menace of personal violence, and every outrage of language, besides disclosing a hideous Barbarism, also discloses the fevered nervousness of a cause already humbled in debate.

(4.) Much as has been said to exhibit the Character of Slave-masters, the work would be incomplete if I failed to point out that *unconsciousness* of the fatal influence of Slavery, which completes the evidence of the Barbarism under which they live. Nor am I at liberty to decline this topic; but I shall be brief.

That Senators should openly declare Slavery "ennobling," at least to the master, and also "the black marble keystone of our national arch," would excite wonder if it were not explained by the examples of history. There are men who, in the spirit of paradox, make themselves the partisans of a bad cause, as Jerome Cardan wrote an Encomium on Nero. But where there is no disposition to paradox, it is natural that a cherished practice should blind those who are under its influence; nor is there any end to these exaggerations. According to Thucydides, piracy in the early ages of Greece was alike widespread and honorable; so much so, that Telemachus and Mentor, on landing at Pylos, were asked by Nestor if they were "pirates"—precisely as a stranger in South-Carolina might be asked if he were a Slave-master. Kidnapping, too, which was a kindred indulgence, was openly avowed, and I doubt not held to be "ennobling." Next to the unconsciousness which is noticed in childhood, is the unconsciousness of Barbarism. The real Barbarian is as unconscious as an infant; and the Slave-master shows much of the same character. No New-Zealander exults in his tattoo, no savage of the North-west coast exults in his flat head, more than the Slave-master in these latter days — and always, of course, with honorable exceptions — exults in his unfortunate condition. The Slave-master hugs his disgusting practice as the Carib of the Gulf hugged Cannibalism, and as Brigham Young now hugs Polygamy. The delusion of the "Goitre" is repeated. This prodigious swelling of the neck, constituting "a hideous wallet of flesh" pendulous upon the breast, is common to the population on the slopes of the Alps; but, accustomed to this deformity, the sufferer comes to regard it with pride, as Slave-masters with us regard Slavery, and it is said that those who have no swelling are laughed at and called " goose-necked."

With knowledge comes distrust and the modest consciousness of imperfection; but the pride of Barbarism has no such limitations. It dilates in the thin air of ignorance, and makes boasts. Surely, if these illustrations are not entirely inapplicable, then must we find in the boasts of Slave-masters new occasion to regret the influence of Slavery.

It is this same influence which renders Slave-masters insensible to those characters which are among the true glories of the Republic; which makes them forget that Jefferson, who wrote the Declaration of Independence, and Washington, who commanded its armies, were Abolitionists; which renders them insensible to the inspiring words of the one, and to the commanding example of the other. Of these great men, it is the praise, well-deserving perpetual mention, and only grudged by a malign influence, that reared amidst Slavery, they did not hesitate to condemn it. To the present debate, Jefferson, in repeated utterances, alive with the fire of genius and truth, has contributed the most important testimony for Freedom ever pronounced in this hemisphere, in words equal to the cause, and Washington, often quoted as a Slave-master, in the solemn dispositions of his last Will and Testament, has contributed an example which is beyond even the words of Jefferson. Do not, sir, call him a Slave-master, who entered into the presence of his Maker only as the Emancipator of his slaves. The difference between such men and the Slave-masters whom I expose to-day is so precise that it can not be mistaken. The first *looked down* upon Slavery; the second *look up* to Slavery. The first, recognizing its wrong, were at once liberated from its pernicious influences, while the latter, upholding it as right and "ennobling," must naturally draw from it motives of conduct. The first, conscious of the character of Slavery, were not misled by it; the second, dwelling in unconsciousness of its true character, surrendered blindly to its barbarous tendencies, and, verifying the words of the poet,

> ———" So perfect is their misery,
> Not once perceive their foul disfigurement,
> But boast themselves more comely than before."

Mr. President, it is time to close this branch of the argument. The Barbarism of Slavery has been now exposed, first, in the Law of Slavery, with its five pretensions, founded on the assertion of property in man, the denial of the conjugal relation, the infraction of the parental relation, the exclusion from knowledge, and the robbery of the fruits of another's labor, all these having the single object of *compelling men to work without wages*, while its Barbarism was still further attested by tracing the law in its origin to barbarous Africa; and secondly, it has been exposed in a careful examination of the economical results of Slavery, illustrated by a contrast between the Free States and the Slave States, sustained by official figures. From this exposure of Slavery, I proceeded to consider its influences on Slave-masters; whose true character stands confessed, first, in the Law of Slavery which is their work; next, in the relations between them and their slaves, maintained by three inhuman instruments; next, in their relations with each other and with society, and here we have seen them at home under the immediate influence of Slavery—also in the communities of which they are a part—practicing violence, and pushing it everywhere, in street-fight and duel; especially raging against all who question the pretensions of Slavery; entering even into the Free States; but not in lawless outbreaks only; also in official acts, as of Georgia and of South-Carolina, with regard to two Massachusetts citizens; and then ascending in audacity, entering the Halls of Congress, where they have raged, as at home, against all who set themselves against their assumptions, while the whole gloomy array of unquestionable facts has been closed by portraying the melancholy unconsciousness which constitutes one of the distinctive features of this Barbarism.

Such is my answer to the assumption of fact in behalf of Slavery by Senators on the other side. But before passing to that other assumption of constitutional law, which constitutes the second branch of this discussion, I add testimony to the influence of Slavery on Slave-masters in other countries, which is too important to be neglected, and may properly find a place here.

Among those who have done most to press forward in Russia that sublime act of emancipation by which the present Emperor is winning lustre, not only for his own country, but for our age, is M. Tourgueneff. Originally a Slave-master himself, with numerous slaves, and residing where Slavery prevailed, he saw, with the instincts of a noble character, the essential Barbarism of this relation, and in an elaborate work on Russia, which is now before me, he exposed it with rare ability and courage. Thus he speaks of its influence on Slave-masters:

> "But if Slavery degrades the slave, it degrades more the master. This is an old adage, and long observations have proved to me that this adage is not a paradox. In fact, how can that man respect his own dignity, his own rights, who has learned not to respect either the rights or the dignity of his fellow-man? What control can the moral and religious sentiments have over a man who sees himself invested with a power so eminently contrary to morals and religion? The continual exercise of an unjust claim, even when it is moderated, finishes by corrupting the character of the man, and spoiling his judgment. . . . . The possession of a slave being the result of injustice, the relations of the master with the slave can not be otherwise than a succession of injustices. Among good masters, (and it is agreed to call so those who do not abuse their power as much as they might,) these relations are clothed with forms less repugnant than among others; but here the difference stops. Who could remain always pure, when, carried away by his disposition, excited by his temper, drawn by caprice, he can with impunity oppress, insult, humiliate his fellows? And, let it be carefully remarked, that intelligence, civilization, do not avail. The enlightened man, the civilized man, is none the less a man; that he should not oppress, it is necessary that it should be impossible for him to oppress. All men can not, like Louis XIV., throw their stick from the window, when they feel a desire to strike."—*La Russie et Les Russes*, Vol. II. pp. 157–58.

Another authority, unimpeachable at all points, whose fortune it has been, from extensive travels, to see Slavery in the most various forms, and Slave-masters under the most various conditions — I refer to the great African traveler, Dr. Livingstone—thus touches the character of Slave-masters:

> "I can never cease to be unfeignedly thankful that I was not born in a land of slaves. No one can understand the unutterable meanness of the slave-system on the minds of those who, *but for the strange obliquity which prevents them from feeling the degradation of not being gentlemen enough to pay for services rendered,* would be equal in virtue to ourselves. Fraud becomes as natural to them 'as paying one's way' is to the rest of mankind."—*Livingstone's Travels,* Chap. II., p. 33.

Thus does the experience of Slavery in other countries confirm the sad experience among us.

SECOND ASSUMPTION.—Discarding now all the presumptuous boasts for Slavery, and bearing in mind its essential Barbarism, I come to consider that second assumption of Senators on the other side, which is, of course, inspired by the first, even if not its immediate consequence, that, under the Constitution, Slave-masters may take their slaves into the national Territories, and there continue to hold them, as at home in the Slave States;

and that this would be the case in any territory newly acquired, by purchase or by war, as of Mexico on the South or Canada on the North.

And here I begin by the remark, that as the assumption of constitutional law is inspired by the assumption of fact with regard to the "ennobling" character of Slavery, so it must lose much if not all of its force when the latter assumption is shown to be false, as has been done to-day.

When Slavery is seen to be the Barbarism which it is, there are few who would not cover it from sight, rather than insist upon sending it abroad with the flag of the Republic. It is only because people have been insensible to its true character that they have tolerated for a moment its exorbitant pretensions. Therefore this long exposition, where Slavery has been made to stand forth in its five-fold Barbarism, with the single object of compelling men to work without wages, naturally prepares the way to consider the assumption of constitutional law.

This assumption may be described as an attempt to *Africanize* the Constitution, by introducing into it the barbarous Law of Slavery, derived as we have seen originally from barbarous Africa; and then, through such *Africanization* of the Constitution, to *Africanize* the Territories, and to *Africanize* the National Government. In using this language to express the obvious effect of this assumption, I borrow a suggestive term, first employed by a Portuguese writer at the beginning of this century, when protesting against the spread of Slavery in Brazil. (See *Koster's Travels in Brazil*, vol. ii. p. 248.) Analyze the assumption, and it will be found to stand on two pretensions, either of which failing, the assumption fails also. These two are—first, the African pretension of property in man; and, secondly, the pretension that such property is recognized in the Constitution.

With regard to the first of these pretensions, I might simply refer to what I have already said at an earlier stage of this argument. But I should do injustice to the part it has been made to play in this controversy, if I did not again expose it. Then I sought particularly to show its Barbarism; now I shall show something more.

Property implies an owner and a thing owned. On the one side is a human being, and on the other side a thing. But the very idea of a human being necessarily excludes the idea of property in that being, just as the very idea of a thing necessarily excludes the idea of a human being. It is clear that a thing can not be a human being, and it is equally clear that a human being can not be a thing. And the law itself, when it adopts the phrase, "relation of master and slave," confesses its reluctance to sanction the claim of property. It shrinks from the pretension of Senators, and satisfies itself with a formula, which does not openly degrade human nature.

If this property does exist, out of what title is it derived? Under what ordinance of Nature or of Nature's God is one human being stamped an owner and another stamped a thing? God is no respecter of persons. Where is the sanction for this respect of certain persons to a degree which becomes outrage to other persons? God is the Father of the Human Family, and we are all his children. Where then is the sanction of this pretension by which a brother lays violent hands upon a brother? To ask these questions is humiliating; but it is clear there can be but one response. There is no sanction for such pretension; no ordinance for it, or title. On all grounds of reason, and waiving all questions of "positive" statute, the Vermont Judge was nobly right, when, rejecting the claim of a Slave-master, he said: "No; not until you show a Bill of Sale from the Almighty." Nothing short of this impossible link in the chain of title would do. I know something of the great judgments by which the jurisprudence of our country has been illustrated; but I doubt if there is any thing in the wisdom of Marshall, the learning of Story, or the completeness of Kent, which will brighten with time like this honest decree.

The intrinsic feebleness of this pretension is apparent in the intrinsic feebleness of the arguments by which it is maintained. These are two-fold, and both have been put forth in recent debate by the Senator from Mississippi, [Mr. DAVIS.]

The first is the alleged inferiority of the African race; an argument which, while surrendering to Slavery a whole race, leaves it uncertain whether the same principle may not be applied to other races, as to the polished Japanese, who are now the guests of the nation, and even to persons of obvious inferiority in the white race. Indeed, the latter pretension is openly made in other quarters. The *Richmond Enquirer*, a leading journal of Slave-masters, declares: "The principle of Slavery is in itself right, and *does not depend on difference of complexion.*" And a leading writer among Slave-masters, George Fitzhugh, of Virginia, in his *Sociology for the South,* declares: "Slavery, *black or white,* is right and necessary. Nature has made the weak in mind or body for slaves." And in the same vein, a Democratic paper of South-Carolina has said: "Slavery is the natural and normal condition of the laboring man, *white or black.*"

These more extravagant pretensions reveal still further the feebleness of the pretension put forth by the Senator; while instances, accumulating constantly, attest the difficulty of discriminating between the two races. Mr. Paxton, of Virginia, tells us, that "the best blood in Virginia flows in the veins of the slaves;" and fugitive slaves have been latterly advertised as possessing "a round face," "blue eyes," "flaxen hair," and as "escaping under the pretense of being a white man."

This is not the time to enter upon the great question of race, in the various lights of religion, history, and science. Sure I am that they who understand it best, will be least disposed to the pretension, which, on the assumed ground of inferiority, would condemn one race to be the property of another. If the African race be inferior, as is alleged, then is it the unquestionable duty of a Christian Civilization to lift it from its degradation, not by the bludgeon and the chain, not by this barbarous pretension of ownership, but by a generous charity, which shall be measured precisely by the extent of its inferiority.

The second argument put forward for this pretension, and twice repeated by the Senator from Mississippi, is, that the Africans are the posterity of Ham, the son of Noah, through Canaan, who was cursed by Noah, to be the "servant"—that is the word employed—of his brethren, and that this malediction has fallen upon all his descendants, who are accordingly devoted by God to perpetual bondage, not only in the third and fourth generations, but throughout all succeeding time. Surely, when the Senator quoted Scripture to enforce the claim of Slave-masters, he did not intend a jest. And yet it is hard to suppose him in earnest. The Senator is Chairman of the Committee on Military Affairs, in which he is doubtless experienced. He may, perhaps, set a squadron in the field, but he has evidently considered very little the text of Scripture on which he relies. The Senator assumes, that it has fixed the doom of the colored race, leaving untouched the white race. Perhaps he does not know that, in the worst days of the Polish aristocracy, this same argument was adopted as the excuse for holding white serfs in bondage, precisely as it is now put forward by the Senator, and that even to this day the angry Polish noble addresses his white peasant as the " son of Ham."

It hardly comports with the gravity of this debate to dwell on such an argument, and yet I can not go wrong if, for the sake of a much-injured race, I brush it away. To justify the Senator in his application of this ancient curse, he must maintain at least five different propositions, as essential links in the chain of the Afric-American slave : *first*, that, by this malediction, Canaan himself was actually changed into a " chattel," whereas he is simply made the "servant" of his brethren ; *secondly*, that not merely Canaan, but all his posterity, to the remotest generation, was so changed, whereas the language has no such extent; *thirdly*, that the Afric-American actually belongs to the posterity of Canaan—an ethnological assumption absurdly difficult to establish ; *fourthly*, that each of the descendants of Shem and Japheth has a right to hold an Afric-American fellow-man as a " chattel "—a proposition which finds no semblance of support ; and *fifthly*, that every Slave-master is truly descended from Shem or Japheth—a pedigree which no anxiety can establish ! This plain analysis, which may fitly excite a smile, shows the five-fold absurdity of an attempt to found this pretension on

> " Any successive title, long and dark,
> Drawn from the mouldy rolls of Noah's ark."

From the character of these two arguments for property in man, I am brought again to its denial.

It is natural that Senators who pretend that, by the law of nature, man may hold property in man, should find this pretension in the Constitution. But the pretension is as much without foundation in the Constitution as it is without foundation in nature. It is not too much to say that there is not one sentence, phrase, or word—not a single suggestion, hint, or equivocation, even—out of which any such pretension can be implied ; while great national acts and important contemporaneous declarations in the Convention which framed the Constitution, in different forms of language, and also controlling rules of interpretation render this pretension impossible. Partisans, taking counsel of their desires, find in the Constitution, as in the Scriptures, what they incline to find; and never was this more apparent than when Slave-masters deceive themselves so far as to find in the Constitution a pretension which exists only in their own souls.

Looking juridically for one moment at this question, we shall be brought to the conclusion, according to the admission of courts and jurists, first in Europe, and then in our own country, that Slavery can be derived from no doubtful word or mere pretension, but only from clear and special recognition. "The state of Slavery," said Lord Mansfield, pronouncing judgment in the great case of Somerset, "is of such a nature that it is incapable of being introduced on any reasons, moral or political, but only by *positive law*. It is so odious, that nothing can be suffered to support it but POSITIVE LAW"—that is, express words of a written text; and this principle, which commends itself to the enlightened reason, has been adopted by several courts in the Slave States. Of course, every leaning must be against Slavery. A pretension so peculiar and offensive — so hostile to reason—so repugnant to the laws of nature and the inborn Rights of Man; which, in all its five-fold wrong, has no other object than to compel fellow-men to work without wages; such a pretension, so tyrannical, so unjust, so mean, so barbarous, can find no place in any system of Government, unless by virtue of *positive sanction*. It can spring from no doubtful phrases. It must be declared by unambiguous words, incapable of a double sense.

At the adoption of the Constitution, this rule, promulgated in the Court of King's Bench, by the voice of the most finished magistrate in English history, was as well known in our country as any principle of the common law; especially was it known to the eminent lawyers in the Convention; nor is it too much to say that the Constitution was framed with this rule on Slavery as a guide. And the Supreme Court of the United States at a later day, in the case of *United States* v. *Fisher*, 2 Cranch, 390, by the voice of Chief-Justice Marshall, promulgated this same rule, in words stronger even than those of Lord Mansfield, saying: "Where rights are infringed, where fundamental principles are overthrown, where the general system of the laws is departed from, the legislative intention must be expressed with *irresistible clearness*, to induce a court of justice to suppose a design to effect such object." It is well known, however, that these two declarations are little more than new forms for the ancient rule of the common law, as expressed by Fortescue: *Impius et crudelis judicandus est qui Libertati non favet:* He is to be adjudged impious and cruel who does not favor Liberty; and, as expressed by Blackstone, " The law is always ready to catch at any thing in favor of Liberty."

But, as no prescription runs against the King, so no prescription is allowed to run against Slavery, while all the early victories of Freedom are set aside by the Slave-masters of to-day. The prohibition of Slavery in the Missouri Territory, and all the precedents, legislative and judicial, for the exercise of this power, admitted from the beginning until now, have been overturned; but at last, bolder grown Slave-masters do not hesitate to assail that principle of jurisprudence which makes Slavery the creature of " positive law " alone, to be upheld only by words of "irresistible clearness." The case of *Somerset*, in which this great rule was declared, has been impeached on this floor, as the Declaration of Independence has been impeached also. And here the Senator from Louisiana [Mr. BENJAMIN] has taken the lead. He has dwelt on the assertion that, in the history of English law, there were earlier cases, where a contrary principle was declared. But permit me to say that no such cases, even if they exist in authentic reports, can impair the influence of this well-considered authority. The Senator knows well that an old and barbarous case is a poor answer to a principle, which is brought into activity by the demands of an advancing Civilization, and which once recognized can never be denied; that jurisprudence is not a dark lantern, shining in a narrow circle, and never changing, but a gladsome light, which, slowly emerging from original darkness, grows and spreads with human improvement, until at last it becomes as broad and general as the Light of Day. When the Senator, in this age—leaguing all his forces—undertakes to drag down that immortal principle, which made Slavery impossible in England, as, thank God! it makes Slavery impossible under the Constitution, he vainly tugs to drag down a luminary from the sky.

The enormity of the pretension that Slavery is sanctioned by the Constitution becomes still more apparent, when we read the Constitution in the light of great national acts and of cotemporaneous declarations. First comes the Declaration of Independence, the illuminated initial letter of our history, which in familiar words announces that "all men are created equal; that they are endowed by their Creator with certain unalienable rights; that among these are Life, *Liberty*, and the Pursuit of Happiness; that to secure these rights governments are instituted among men, deriving their just powers from the consent of the governed." Nor does this Declaration, binding the consciences of all who enjoy the privileges it secured, stand alone. There is another national act, less known, but in itself a key to the first, when, at the successful close of the Revolution, the Continental Congress, in a solemn address to the people, loftily announced: " Let it be remembered, that it has ever been the pride and the boast of America, *that the rights for which she has contended were the rights of human nature.* By the blessing of the Author of *these rights*, they have prevailed over all opposition, and form THE BASIS of thirteen independent States." Now, whatever may be the privileges of States in their individual capacities, within their several local jurisdictions, no power can be attributed to the nation, in the absence of positive unequivocal grant, inconsistent with these two national declarations. Here is the national heart, the national soul, the national will, the national voice, which must inspire our interpretation of the Constitution, and enter into and diffuse itself through all the national legislation. Such are the commanding authorities which constitute "Life, Liberty, and the Pursuit of Happiness," and in more general words, "the Rights of Human Nature," without distinction of race, or recognition of the curse of Ham, as the basis of our national institutions. They need no additional support.

But in strict harmony with these are the many utterances in the Convention which framed the Constitution: of Gouverneur Morris, of Pennsylvania, who announced that "*he would never concur in upholding domestic Slavery; it was a nefarious institution;*" of Elbridge Gerry, of Massachusetts, who said "that we had nothing to do with the conduct of the States as to Slavery, *but we ought to be careful not to give any sanction to it;*" of Roger Sherman and Oliver Ellsworth, of Connecticut, and Mr. Gorham,

74

of Massachusetts, who all concurred with Mr. Gerry; and especially of Mr. Madison, of Virginia, who, in mild juridical phrase, "THOUGHT IT WRONG TO ADMIT IN THE CONSTITUTION THE IDEA THAT THERE COULD BE PROPERTY IN MAN." And lastly, as if to complete the elaborate work of Freedom, and to give expression to all these utterances, the word "servitude," which had been allowed in the clause on the apportionment of Representatives, was struck out, and the word "service" substituted instead. This final exclusion from the Constitution of the idea of property in man was on the motion of Mr. Randolph, of Virginia; and the reason assigned for the substitution, according to Mr. Madison, in his authentic report of the debate, was, that "the former was thought to express the condition of slaves, and the latter *the obligations of free persons.*" Thus, at every point, by great national declarations, by frank utterances in the Convention, and by a positive act in adjusting the text of the Constitution, was the idea of property in man unequivocally rejected.

This pretension, which may be dismissed as utterly baseless, becomes absurd when it is considered to what result it necessarily conducts. If the Barbarism of Slavery, in all its five-fold wrong, is really embodied in the Constitution, so as to be beyond the reach of prohibition, either Congressional or local, in the Territories, then, for the same reason, it must be beyond the reach of prohibition or abolition, even by local authority in the States themselves, and just so long as the Constitution continues unchanged, Territories and States alike must be open to all its blasting influences. And yet this pretension, which, in its natural consequences, overturns State Rights, is put forward by Senators, who profess to be the special guardians of State Rights.

Nor does this pretension derive any support from the much-debated clause in the Constitution for the rendition of fugitives from "service or labor," on which so much stress is constantly put. But I do not occupy your time now on this head, for two reasons—first, because, having already on a former occasion exhibited with great fullness the character of that clause, I am unwilling now thus incidentally to open the question upon it; and secondly, because, whatever may be its character—admitting that it confers power upon Congress—and admitting also, what is often denied, that, in defiance of commanding rules of interpretation, the equivocal words there employed have that "irresistible clearness" which is necessary in taking away Human Rights—yet nothing can be clearer than that the fugitives, whosoever they may be, are regarded under the Constitution as *persons*, and not as *property*.

I disdain to dwell on that other argument, brought forward by Senators, who, denying the Equality of Man, speciously assert the Equality of the States; and from this principle, true in many respects, jump to the conclusion, that Slave-masters are entitled, in the name of Equality, to take their slaves into the National Territories, under the solemn safeguards of the Constitution. But this argument comes back to the first pretension, that slaves are recognized as "property" in the Constitution. To that pretension, already amply exposed, we are always brought, nor can any sounding allegations of State Equality avoid it. And yet this very argument betrays the inconsistency of its authors. If persons held to service in the Slave States are "property" under the Constitution, then under the provision—known as the "three fifths" rule—which founds representation in the other House on such persons, there is a *property representation* from the Slave States, with voice and vote, while there is no such *property representation* from the Free States. With glaring inequality, the representation of Slave States is founded first on "persons," and secondly on a large part of their pretended property; while the representation of the Free States is founded simply on "persons," leaving all their boundless millions of property unrepresented. Thus, whichever way we approach it, the absurdity of this pretension becomes manifest. Assuming the pretension of property in man under the Constitution, you slap in the face the whole theory of State Equality, for you disclose a gigantic inequality between the Slave States and the Free States; and assuming the Equality of States, in the House of Representatives as elsewhere, you slap in the face the whole pretension of property in man under the Constitution.

I disdain to dwell also on that other argument, which, in the name of Popular Sovereignty, undertakes to secure to the people in the Territories the wicked power—sometimes called, by confusion of terms, right—to enslave their fellow-men; as if this pretension was not blasted at once by the Declaration of Independence, when it announced that "all governments derive their just powers from the consent of the governed," and as if anywhere within the jurisdiction of the Constitution, which contains no sentence, phrase, or word, sanctioning this outrage, and which carefully excludes the idea of property in man, while it surrounds all persons with the highest safeguards of a citizen, such pretension could exist. Whatever it may be elsewhere, Popular Sovereignty within the sphere of the Constitution has its limitations. Claiming for all the largest liberty of a true Civilization, it compresses all within the constraints of Justice; nor does it allow any man to assert a right to do what he pleases, except when he pleases to do right. As well within the Territories attempt to make a King as attempt to make a slave. But this pretension—rejected alike by every Slave-master and by every lover of Freedom—

> Where I behold a factious band agree
> To call it freedom when themselves are free,

proceeding originally from a vain effort to avoid the impending question between Freedom and Slavery—assuming a delusive phrase of Freedom as a cloak for Slavery—speaking with the voice of Jacob while its hands are the hands of Esau—and, by its plausible nick-name, enabling politicians sometimes to deceive the public, and sometimes even to deceive themselves—may be dismissed with the other kindred pretensions for Slavery, while the Senator from Illinois, [Mr. DOUGLAS,] who, if not its inventor, has been its boldest defender, will learn that Slave-masters, for whom he has done so much, can not afford to be generous; that their gratitude is founded on what they expect, and not on what they have received; and, that having its root in desire rather than in fruition, it necessarily withers and dies with the power to serve them. The Senator, revolving these things in his mind, may confess the difficulty of his position, and, perhaps,

> ——— remember Milo's end,
> Wedged in that Timber which he strove to rend.

And here I close this branch of the argument, which I have treated less fully than the first, partly because time and strength fail me, but chiefly because the Barbarism of Slavery, when fully established, supersedes all other inquiry. But enough has been done on this head. At the risk of repetition, I now gather it together. The assumption that Slave-masters, under the Constitution, may take their slaves into the Territories, and continue to hold them as in the States, stands on two pretensions—first, that man may hold property in man, and, secondly, that this property is recognized in the Constitution. But we have seen that the pretended property in man stands on no reason, while the two special arguments by which it has been asserted, first an alleged inferiority of race, and secondly the ancient curse of Ham, are grossly insufficient to uphold such a pretension. And we have next seen that this pretension has as little support in the Constitution as in reason; that Slavery is of such an offensive character, that it can find support only in "positive" sanction, and words of "irresistible clearness;" that this benign rule, questioned in the Senate, is consistent with the principles of an advanced civilization; that no such "positive" sanction, in words of "irresistible clearness," can be found in the Constitution, while, in harmony with the Declaration of Independence, and the Address of the Continental Congress, the cotemporaneous declarations in the Convention, and especially the act of the Convention in substituting "service" for "servitude," on the ground that the latter expressed "the condition of slaves," all attest that the pretension that man can hold property in man was carefully, scrupulously, and completely excluded from the Constitution, so that it has no semblance of support in that sacred text; nor is this pretension, which is unsupported in the Constitution, helped by the two arguments, one in the name of State Equality, and the other in the name of Popular Sovereignty, both of which are properly put aside.

Sir, the true principle, which, reversing the assumptions of Slave-masters, makes Freedom *national* and Slavery *sectional*, while every just claim of the Slave States is harmonized with the irresistible predominance of Freedom under the Constitution, has been declared at Chicago. Not questioning the right of each State, whether South-Carolina or Turkey, Virginia or Russia, to order and control its own domestic institutions according to its own judgment exclusively, the Convention there assembled has explicitly announced Freedom to be "the normal condition of all the Territory of the United States," and has explicitly denied "the authority of Congress, of a Territorial Legislature, or of any individuals, to give legal existence to Slavery in any Territory of the United States." Such is the triumphant response by the aroused millions of the North, alike to the assumption of Slave-masters that the Constitution, of its own force, carries Slavery into the Territories, and also to the device of politicians, that the people of the Territories, in the exercise of a dishonest Popular Sovereignty, may plant Slavery there. This response is complete at all points, whether the Constitution acts upon the Territories before their organization, or only afterward; for, in the absence of a Territorial Government, there can be no "positive" law in words of "irresistible clearness" for Slavery, as there can be no such law, when a Territorial Government is organized, under the Constitution. Thus the normal condition of the Territories is confirmed by the Constitution, which, when extended over them, renders Slavery impossible, while it writes upon the soil and engraves upon the rock everywhere the law of impartial Freedom, without distinction of color or race.

Mr. President, this argument is now closed. Pardon me for the time I have occupied. It is long since I have made any such claim upon your attention. Pardon me, also, if I have said any thing which I ought not to have said. I have spoken frankly and from the heart; if severely, yet only with the severity of a sorrowful candor, calling things by their right names, and letting historic facts tell their unimpeachable story. I have spoken in the patriotic hope of contributing to the welfare of my country, and also in the assured conviction that what I have said will find a response in generous souls. I believe that I have said nothing which is not sustained by well-founded argument or well-founded testimony, nothing which can be controverted without a direct assault upon reason or upon truth.

The two assumptions of Slave-masters have been answered. But this is not enough. Let the answer become a legislative act, by the admission of Kansas as a Free State. Then will the Barbarism of Slavery be repelled, and the pretension of property in man be rebuked. Such an act, closing this long struggle by the assurance of peace to the Territory, if not of tranquillity to the whole country, will be more grateful still as the herald of that better day, near at hand, when Freedom shall be installed everywhere under the National Government; when the National Flag, wherever it floats, on sea or land, within the national jurisdiction, will not cover a single slave; and when the Declaration of Independence, now reviled in the name of Slavery, will once again be reverenced as the American Magna Charta of Human Rights. Nor is this all. Such an act will be the first stage in those triumphs by which the Republic— lifted in character so as to become an example to mankind—will enter at last upon its noble " prerogative of teaching the nations how to live."

Thus, sir, speaking for Freedom in Kansas, I have spoken for Freedom everywhere, and for Civilization; and, as the less is contained in the greater, so are all arts, all sciences, all econo- mies, all refinements, all charities, all delights of life, embodied in this cause. You may reject it; but it will be only for to-day. The sacred animosity between Freedom and Slavery can end only with the triumph of Freedom. This same Question will be soon carried before that high tribunal, supreme over Senate and Court, where the judges will be counted by millions, and where the judgment rendered will be the solemn charge of an aroused people, instructing a new President, in the name of Freedom, to see that Civilization receives no detriment.

When Mr. SUMNER resumed his seat, Mr. CHESNUT, of South- Carolina, spoke as follows:

Mr. President, after the extraordinary though characteristic speech just uttered in the Senate, it is proper that I assign the reason for the position we are now in- clined to assume. After ranging over Europe, crawling through the back-doors to whine at the feet of British aristocracy, craving pity, and reaping a rich harvest of contempt, the slanderer of States and men reäppears in the Senate. We had hoped to be relieved from the outpourings of such vulgar malice. We had hoped that one who had felt, though ignominiously he failed to meet, the consequences of a former insolence, would have become wiser, if not better, by experience. In this I am disappointed, and I regret it. Mr. President, in the heroic ages of the world, men were deified for the possession and the exercise of some virtues—wisdom, truth, justice, magnanimity, courage. In Egypt, also, we know they deified beasts and reptiles; but even that bestial people worshipped their idols on account of some supposed virtue. It has been left for this day, for this country, for the Abo- litionists of Massachusetts, *to deify the incarnation of malice, mendacity, and cow- ardice.* Sir, we not intend to be guilty of aiding in the apotheosis of pusillanimity and meanness. We do not intend to contribute, by any conduct on our part, to increase the devotees at the shrine of this new idol. We know what is expected and what is desired. *We are not inclined again to send forth the recipient of PUN-*

80

ISHMENT *howling through the world, yelping fresh cries of slander and malice. These are the reasons*, which I feel it due to myself and others to give to the Senate and the country, why we have quietly listened to what has been said, and why we can take no other notice of the matter.

In these words, Mr. Chesnut refers to the assault upon Mr. SUM-NER with a bludgeon on the floor of the Senate, by a Representative from South-Carolina, since dead, aided by another Representative from that same State, and also a Representative from Virginia, on account of which Mr. SUMNER had been compelled to leave his seat vacant, and seek the restoration of his health by travel. As Mr. CHESNUT spoke, he was surrounded by the Slave-masters of the Senate, who seemed to approve what he said. There was no call to order by the Chair, which was occupied at the time by Mr. BIGLER, of Pennsylvania. Mr. SUMNER obtained the floor with difficulty, while a motion was pending for the postponement of the question, and said:

Mr. President, before this question passes away, I think I ought to make (though perhaps there is no occasion for it) a response to the Senator from South-Carolina. ["No!" from several Senators.] Only one word. I exposed to-day the *Barbarism of Slavery.* What the Senator has said in reply to me, I may well print in an Appendix to my speech as an additional illustration. That is all.

Mr. HAMMOND, of South-Carolina, said:

I hope he will do it.

––––––

The following letter, from a venerable citizen, an ornament of our legislative halls at the beginning of the century, and now the oldest survivor of all who have ever been members of Congress, is too valuable, in its testimony and its counsel, to be omitted in this place:

BOSTON, June 5, 1860.

DEAR SIR: I have read a few abstracts from your noble speech, but must wait for it in a pamphlet form, that I may read it in such type as eyes, in the eighty-ninth year of their age, will permit. But I have read enough to approve, and rejoice that you have been permitted, thus truly, fully, and faithfully to expose the "Barbarism" of Slavery on that very floor on which you were so cruelly and brutally stricken down by the spirit of that Barbarism.

I only hope that in an Appendix you will preserve the *vera effigies* of that insect that attempted to sting you. Remember that the value of amber is increased by the insect it preserves. Yours, very truly,

JOSIAH QUINCY.